I0012784

AI Revolution

Introduction to Artificial Intelligence

Table of Contents

CHAPTER 1

What is Artificial Intelligence?

Artificial Intelligence (AI) is the simulation of human intelligence in machines programmed to think and act like humans. It involves developing computer systems that can perform tasks that typically require human intelligence, such as learning, reasoning, problem-solving, perception, and language understanding.

Definition of AI

The definition of AI encompasses a broad range of capabilities, including understanding natural language, recognizing patterns, and making data-based decisions. AI systems can be designed to operate autonomously or to assist human users in various tasks. The goal of AI is to create systems that can perform tasks that would normally require human intelligence.

History of AI

The history of AI dates back decades, with myths and stories about artificial beings with human-like capabilities. However, the modern development of AI as a field of study began in the 1950s. Early AI research focused on symbolic methods, in which computers were programmed to manipulate symbols to solve problems. Over time, AI research has evolved to incorporate statistical methods, machine learning, and neural networks.

Types of AI

AI can be categorized into different types based on its capabilities and limitations. The three main types of AI are Narrow AI, General AI, and Superintelligent AI.

Narrow AI

Narrow AI, also known as Weak AI, is designed to perform a specific or narrow range of tasks. These AI systems are focused on a particular problem and cannot generalize beyond their specific domain. Examples of narrow AI include virtual personal assistants, recommendation systems, and image recognition software.

General AI

General AI, or Strong AI, aims to exhibit human-like intelligence and cognitive abilities. These AI systems can understand, learn, and apply knowledge across various tasks and domains. However, general AI remains a theoretical concept and has not been achieved in practice.

Superintelligent AI

Superintelligent AI refers to AI systems that surpass human intelligence in virtually every area, including scientific creativity, general wisdom, and social skills. The development of superintelligent AI raises significant ethical and existential concerns, as it could potentially outperform humans in decision-making and problem-solving.

How AI Works

AI systems utilize various techniques and approaches to perform intelligent tasks. These include machine learning, deep learning, neural networks, natural language processing, and computer vision.

Machine Learning

Machine learning is a subset of AI that enables systems to learn and improve from experience without being explicitly programmed. It involves using algorithms and statistical models to enable machines to improve their performance on a specific task progressively.

Deep Learning

Deep learning is a specialized form of machine learning that uses neural networks with multiple layers to learn data representations. It has been particularly successful in image and speech recognition.

Neural Networks

Neural networks are a key component of AI. Inspired by the structure and function of the human brain, they consist of interconnected nodes, or "neurons," that work together to process and analyze complex data.

Natural Language Processing

Natural language processing (NLP) focuses on enabling machines to understand, interpret, and respond to human language. NLP techniques are used in language translation, sentiment analysis, and chatbots.

Computer Vision

Computer vision involves developing algorithms and techniques to enable machines to interpret and understand the visual world. This includes object recognition, image classification, and video analysis.

Review Questions

1. What is Artificial Intelligence?

    A. The simulation of human intelligence processes by machines

    B. The study of computer programming

    C. The study of human intelligence and behavior

    D. The study of animal intelligence

2. Which of the following is a type of AI?

    A. Machine Learning

    B. Network Security

    C. Software Development

    D. Data Analysis

3. What is the focus of Natural Language Processing in AI?

    A. Analyzing and interpreting human language

    B. Analyzing and interpreting computer code

    C. Analyzing and interpreting mathematical equations

    D. Analyzing and interpreting visual data

4. Which of the following is a component of how AI works?

A. Electrical Engineering

B. Machine Learning

C. Civil Engineering

D. Hardware Engineering

5. What is the purpose of Neural Networks in AI?

A. Analyzing and interpreting mathematical equations

B. Analyzing and interpreting visual data

C. Recognizing patterns and making decisions

D. Analyzing and interpreting human language

CHAPTER 2

Benefits of AI in Business

Streamlining Operations

Artificial Intelligence (AI) has revolutionized how businesses streamline their operations by automating repetitive tasks, leveraging predictive analytics, and optimizing supply chains. By harnessing the power of AI, organizations can achieve greater efficiency, cost savings, and agility in their day-to-day processes.

Automating Repetitive Tasks

One key benefit of AI in business is the ability to automate repetitive tasks that are time-consuming and prone to human error. AI-powered robotic process automation (RPA) tools allow companies to offload mundane activities such as data entry, invoice processing, and report generation to intelligent software agents. This frees up valuable human resources to focus on more strategic initiatives and ensures consistent and accurate execution of routine operations.

For example, in the finance sector, AI-driven RPA can automate the reconciliation of financial transactions, reducing the manual effort required and minimizing the risk of discrepancies. Similarly, in manufacturing, AI-powered robots can handle repetitive assembly line tasks with precision and speed, leading to enhanced productivity and quality control.

Predictive Analytics

AI empowers businesses to harness the potential of predictive analytics, enabling them to anticipate future trends, customer behaviors, and market dynamics. By leveraging advanced machine learning algorithms, organizations can analyze historical data, identify patterns, and make informed predictions about various aspects of their operations. This proactive approach to decision-making allows businesses to stay ahead of the curve and adapt to changing market conditions.

For instance, AI-driven predictive analytics in retail can forecast consumer demand for specific products, optimizing inventory management and minimizing stockouts. In the healthcare industry, AI-powered predictive analytics can help hospitals and healthcare providers anticipate patient admission rates, enabling them to allocate resources efficiently and improve patient care.

Supply Chain Optimization

AI is pivotal in optimizing supply chain management by enhancing visibility, efficiency, and responsiveness across the entire supply network. By applying AI-driven algorithms and data analytics, businesses can gain real-time insights into their supply chain operations, identify potential bottlenecks, and optimize inventory levels, procurement, and logistics.

For example, AI-powered demand forecasting can enable companies to predict customer demand accurately, leading to optimized production schedules and reduced inventory holding costs. Additionally, AI-based supply chain optimization tools can dynamically adjust transportation routes and distribution networks based on real-time factors such as weather conditions, traffic patterns, and demand fluctuations, ensuring timely and cost-effective delivery of goods.

Enhancing Customer Experience

AI has transformed how businesses interact with their customers, offering personalized recommendations, intelligent chatbots, and sophisticated customer behavior analysis. By leveraging AI technologies, organizations can deliver tailored experiences, improve customer satisfaction, and gain valuable insights into consumer preferences and behaviors.

Personalized Recommendations

AI-powered recommendation systems have become a cornerstone of enhancing the customer experience across various industries, from e-commerce and entertainment to hospitality and finance. By analyzing customer data, purchase history, and browsing patterns, AI algorithms can deliver personalized product recommendations, content suggestions, and promotional offers that resonate with individual preferences and interests.

For instance, leading e-commerce platforms utilize AI to provide personalized product recommendations based on a customer's past purchases, product views, and demographic information. This enhances the customer's shopping experience and drives higher conversion rates and customer loyalty.

Chatbots and Virtual Assistants

AI-powered chatbots and virtual assistants have redefined customer engagement by providing users with instant, personalized, and round-the-clock support. These intelligent conversational agents can understand natural language, resolve customer queries, and even execute transactions, thereby enhancing the overall customer service experience.

For example, in the banking sector, AI-driven chatbots can assist customers with account inquiries, fund transfers, and loan applications, offering seamless and efficient interactions. In the hospitality industry, AI-powered virtual assistants can handle room bookings, provide local recommendations, and address guest inquiries, elevating patrons' service and convenience.

Customer Behavior Analysis

AI enables businesses to gain deep insights into customer behavior and preferences through advanced analytics and machine learning models. Organizations can understand customer sentiment, identify emerging trends, and tailor their offerings to meet evolving consumer needs by analyzing diverse data sources such as social media interactions, website engagement metrics, and purchase histories.

For instance, AI-driven sentiment analysis tools can help businesses gauge public opinion and perception of their products or services, allowing them to fine-tune their marketing strategies and brand messaging. In the telecommunications industry, AI-powered customer behavior analysis can identify patterns in usage data, enabling providers to offer personalized service plans and promotions that align with individual usage patterns and preferences.

Improving Decision Making

AI empowers businesses to make data-driven decisions by providing valuable insights, risk management capabilities, and accurate market forecasting. By leveraging AI technologies, organizations can enhance their strategic planning, mitigate risks, and capitalize on emerging opportunities in a dynamic business environment.

Data-Driven Insights

AI-driven analytics and business intelligence tools enable organizations to extract actionable insights from vast volumes of data, empowering decision-makers to understand trends, identify correlations, and make informed strategic choices. By leveraging AI algorithms, businesses can uncover hidden patterns and relationships within their data, leading to more effective decision-making.

For example, in marketing, AI-powered analytics can provide detailed insights into customer segmentation, campaign performance, and attribution modeling, enabling marketers to optimize their strategies and allocate resources more effectively. In finance, AI-driven data analytics can identify potential investment opportunities, assess market risks, and optimize portfolio management strategies.

Risk Management

AI plays a crucial role in risk management by enabling businesses to identify, assess, and mitigate potential risks across various operational domains. By applying AI-driven predictive modeling and scenario analysis, organizations can proactively manage risks related to financial volatility, supply chain disruptions, cybersecurity threats, and regulatory compliance.

For instance, AI-powered risk assessment models in the insurance sector can evaluate policyholder data, claims history, and external risk factors to calculate precise underwriting and pricing strategies. Similarly, in cybersecurity, AI-driven threat detection and response systems can analyze network traffic patterns, identify anomalous behavior, and thwart potential security breaches in real-time.

Market Forecasting

AI facilitates accurate and timely market forecasting by analyzing historical data, economic indicators, and consumer trends to predict future market dynamics and opportunities. By leveraging machine learning algorithms and predictive modeling, businesses can anticipate shifts in demand, competitive landscapes, and industry trends, enabling them to adapt their strategies and capitalize on emerging market conditions.

For example, in the retail sector, AI-powered demand forecasting can help businesses optimize inventory levels, pricing strategies, and promotional activities based on anticipated consumer demand patterns. In the financial services industry, AI-driven market forecasting can assist investment firms in identifying potential market trends, evaluating asset performance, and optimizing trading strategies.

Increasing Productivity

AI enhances business productivity by automating workflows, optimizing resource allocation, and monitoring performance metrics. By leveraging AI technologies, organizations can streamline operations, maximize efficiency, and drive continuous improvement across their business processes.

Workflow Automation

AI-powered workflow automation tools enable businesses to streamline and optimize their operational processes by automating repetitive tasks, standardizing procedures, and orchestrating complex workflows. By leveraging AI-driven automation, organizations can reduce manual intervention, minimize errors, and accelerate task execution.

For example, in human resources, AI-driven workflow automation can streamline the employee onboarding process, automate leave management, and facilitate performance appraisal workflows, leading to greater operational efficiency and employee satisfaction. In marketing, AI-powered automation can orchestrate multi-channel campaign execution, personalized content delivery, and lead nurturing activities, driving higher marketing productivity and campaign effectiveness.

Efficient Resource Allocation

AI facilitates efficient resource allocation by analyzing data, demand patterns, and operational constraints to optimize the utilization of human capital, financial resources, and infrastructure. By leveraging AI-driven optimization algorithms, businesses can allocate resources to maximize productivity, minimize waste, and align with strategic objectives.

For instance, in project management, AI-powered resource allocation tools can optimize project schedules, allocate human resources based on skill sets and availability, and balance workloads across teams, improving project efficiency and timely delivery. Similarly, AI-driven resource allocation in manufacturing can optimize production schedules, minimize downtime, and ensure optimal utilization of machinery and labor resources.

Performance Monitoring

AI enables businesses to monitor and analyze performance metrics across various operational domains, providing real-time insights into productivity, quality, and operational efficiency. Organizations can identify bottlenecks, track key performance indicators, and drive continuous improvement initiatives by leveraging AI-driven analytics and performance monitoring tools.

For example, in customer service, AI-powered performance monitoring can analyze call center metrics, customer satisfaction scores, and service response times, enabling businesses to optimize service delivery and enhance customer experience. In logistics, AI-driven performance monitoring can track delivery times, route efficiency, and inventory accuracy, improving operational performance and cost savings.

Review Questions

1. Which of the following is a benefit of AI in business for streamlining operations?

    A. Automating Repetitive Tasks

    B. Personalized Recommendations

    C. Risk Management

2. What is a way in which AI enhances customer experience in business?

    A. Workflow Automation

    B. Chatbots and Virtual Assistants

    C. Market Forecasting

3. How does AI contribute to improving decision-making in business?

    A. Efficient Resource Allocation

    B. Data-Driven Insights

    C. Supply Chain Optimization

4. Which aspect of AI in business helps in increasing productivity?

    A. Performance Monitoring

    B. Predictive Analytics

    C. Customer Behavior Analysis

5. What is a key function of AI in business for improving decision making?

    A. Automating Repetitive Tasks

    B. Personalized Recommendations

    C. Risk Management

CHAPTER 3

Benefits of AI in Finance

Risk Management

AI has revolutionized risk management in the financial industry by enabling more sophisticated and efficient methods of identifying and mitigating risks. One of the key areas where AI has made a significant impact is fraud detection. Traditional rule-based systems for detecting fraudulent activities often struggle to keep up with fraudsters' evolving tactics. AI, particularly machine learning algorithms, can analyze large volumes of transactional data and identify patterns indicative of fraudulent behavior. By continuously learning from new data, AI-powered fraud detection systems can adapt to new fraud patterns and improve accuracy over time.

Another critical aspect of risk management where AI has proven invaluable is credit scoring. Traditional credit scoring models rely on a limited set of variables and may not capture the full picture of an individual's creditworthiness. On the other hand, AI algorithms can analyze a wide range of data points, including non-traditional sources such as social media and online behavior, to assess an individual's credit risk more accurately. This can potentially expand access to credit for individuals who traditional scoring models may have overlooked.

Furthermore, AI has been increasingly used in algorithmic trading, where complex algorithms analyze market data and execute trades at high speeds. These algorithms can identify trading opportunities, manage risk, and execute orders with minimal human intervention. AI's ability to process vast amounts of data and make split-second decisions has transformed the trading landscape, increasing efficiency and liquidity in financial markets.

Customer Service and Support

The application of AI in finance has also enhanced customer service and support capabilities. Automated customer assistance, powered by AI-driven chatbots and virtual assistants, has enabled financial institutions to provide round-the-clock customer support. These AI systems can handle a wide range of customer inquiries, from account balance inquiries to transaction disputes, with high accuracy and efficiency. By automating routine customer interactions, financial institutions can free up human agents to focus on more complex and high-value customer needs.

Moreover, AI has enabled the delivery of personalized financial advice to customers. By analyzing individual financial data and behavior, AI systems can offer tailored investment strategies, savings goals, and financial planning recommendations. This level of personalization can significantly improve the customer experience and help individuals make more informed financial decisions.

Transaction monitoring is another area where AI has had a transformative impact. AI-powered systems can analyze large volumes of transactional data in real time to detect unusual patterns or anomalies that may indicate fraudulent activity or compliance violations. This proactive monitoring capability helps financial institutions identify and address potential issues before they escalate, thereby enhancing the security and integrity of financial transactions.

Data Analysis and Insights

AI has empowered financial institutions with advanced data analysis and insights capabilities, enabling them to extract valuable information from vast and complex datasets. Market trends analysis, for instance, has been revolutionized by AI algorithms that can process and interpret large volumes of market data to identify patterns, correlations, and emerging trends. This insight is invaluable for making informed investment decisions and developing effective trading strategies.

Portfolio management has also benefited from AI-driven data analysis. AI systems can analyze historical performance, market conditions, and individual investor preferences to optimize investment portfolios and manage risk more effectively. By leveraging AI's ability to process and analyze diverse data sources, financial professionals can make more informed and data-driven decisions to achieve better portfolio outcomes.

Furthermore, predictive modeling powered by AI has become an essential tool for financial institutions to forecast future market conditions, customer behaviors, and financial risks. By analyzing historical data and identifying patterns, AI models can generate predictive insights that help financial institutions anticipate market movements, customer needs, and potential risks, enabling them to make proactive and strategic decisions.

Regulatory Compliance

Regulatory compliance is a critical aspect of the financial industry, and AI has played a significant role in automating and enhancing compliance processes. AI systems have enabled automated reporting, which has streamlined the generation and submission of regulatory reports, reducing the time and resources required for compliance activities. AI-powered reporting systems can extract relevant data from internal systems, analyze it for compliance requirements, and generate accurate and timely reports, ensuring adherence to regulatory obligations.

AI has also strengthened compliance monitoring, with systems capable of continuously monitoring transactions, communications, and other activities for compliance violations. AI algorithms can detect anomalies, flag potential issues, and provide alerts to compliance teams, enabling proactive intervention to address compliance risks. This real-time monitoring capability is essential for maintaining regulatory compliance in a rapidly evolving financial landscape.

Additionally, AI has facilitated audit trail analysis by automating the process of tracking and analyzing transactional data to ensure transparency and accountability. AI-powered systems can efficiently trace the flow of financial transactions, identify irregularities, and provide comprehensive audit trails that support regulatory audits and investigations, thereby enhancing the integrity and trustworthiness of financial operations.

Review Questions

1. Which of the following is a benefit of AI in finance related to identifying and preventing fraudulent activities?

    A. Market Trends Analysis

    B. Automated Reporting

    C. Fraud Detection

    D. Personalized Financial Advice

2. What aspect of finance does AI help with by providing personalized financial advice to customers?

    A. Credit Scoring

    B. Transaction Monitoring

    C. Automated Customer Assistance

    D. Personalized Financial Advice

3. In finance, which AI application involves analyzing market trends and making predictions based on the data?

    A. Compliance Monitoring

    B. Portfolio Management

    C. Predictive Modeling

    D. Market Trends Analysis

4. Which AI application in finance focuses on ensuring adherence to regulatory requirements and standards?

    A. Algorithmic Trading

    B. Audit Trail Analysis

    C. Transaction Monitoring

    D. Automated Customer Assistance

5. How does AI support risk management in finance by evaluating the creditworthiness of individuals and businesses?

    A. Fraud Detection

    B. Personalized Financial Advice

    C. Credit Scoring

    D. Automated Reporting

CHAPTER 4

Benefits of AI in Manufacturing

Process Optimization

Process optimization is a critical aspect of manufacturing, and AI significantly enhances this optimization. By leveraging AI technologies, manufacturers can achieve several benefits in process optimization.

Predictive Maintenance

Predictive maintenance is a proactive approach that uses AI algorithms to predict when equipment failure might occur. By analyzing historical and real-time sensor data, AI can identify patterns and anomalies that indicate potential issues with machinery or equipment. This allows manufacturers to schedule maintenance activities at opportune times, reducing downtime and preventing costly breakdowns.

Furthermore, predictive maintenance can reduce costs by extending equipment's lifespan and reducing the need for emergency repairs. It also contributes to overall operational efficiency and productivity by ensuring that machinery functions optimally.

Quality Control

Quality control is a critical aspect of manufacturing, ensuring that products meet the required standards and specifications. AI-powered quality control systems can analyze large volumes of data from production processes to identify defects, deviations, or irregularities in real-time. Using machine learning algorithms, these systems can continuously learn and improve their ability to detect and address quality issues.

AI-driven quality control enhances inspection consistency and accuracy and enables early detection of potential defects, reducing waste and rework. This ultimately leads to improved product quality and customer satisfaction.

Supply Chain Management

AI technologies have revolutionized supply chain management in the manufacturing industry. Manufacturers can achieve greater efficiency and responsiveness in their supply chain operations by leveraging AI for demand forecasting, inventory optimization, and logistics planning.

Machine learning algorithms can analyze historical sales data, market trends, and other relevant factors to more accurately predict demand. This enables manufacturers to optimize inventory levels, reduce stockouts, and minimize excess inventory. Additionally, AI-powered supply chain management systems can identify potential disruptions and provide recommendations for mitigating risks, thereby enhancing the supply chain's resilience.

Product Innovation

Product innovation is essential for manufacturers to stay competitive in the market, and AI offers numerous opportunities to drive innovation across various stages of product development and manufacturing.

Design Optimization

AI optimizes design by leveraging advanced algorithms to analyze complex design parameters, performance requirements, and material characteristics. By using generative design algorithms, engineers can explore a wide range of design options and identify optimal solutions that meet specific criteria, such as weight reduction, structural integrity, or manufacturing constraints.

Furthermore, AI can facilitate the integration of design and manufacturing processes, enabling seamless collaboration between design teams and production facilities. This integration can lead to innovative and manufacturable designs, ultimately accelerating the product development cycle.

Smart Manufacturing

Smart manufacturing, also known as Industry 4.0, involves integrating advanced technologies, including AI, IoT, and robotics, to create highly automated and interconnected production systems. AI plays a central role in smart manufacturing by enabling real-time data analysis, predictive analytics, and adaptive control of manufacturing processes.

By implementing AI-driven smart manufacturing systems, manufacturers can achieve greater flexibility, agility, and responsiveness in their production operations. These systems can optimize production schedules, minimize downtime, and adapt to changing demand or production requirements, ultimately improving operational efficiency and cost savings.

Customization and Personalization

AI technologies enable manufacturers to offer customized and personalized products to meet customers' diverse needs and preferences. Using AI-driven design tools, manufacturers can create customizable product configurations and variations without compromising production efficiency.

Furthermore, AI-powered recommendation systems can analyze customer data and preferences to provide personalized product recommendations, enhancing customer satisfaction and loyalty. This level of customization and personalization can differentiate manufacturers in the market and drive competitive advantage.

Resource Management

Efficient resource management, including energy, inventory, and workforce, is crucial for the sustainability and competitiveness of manufacturing operations. AI offers several capabilities to optimize resource management in manufacturing.

Energy Efficiency

AI-based energy management systems can analyze energy consumption patterns, identify opportunities for energy savings, and optimize the operation of energy-intensive equipment. By leveraging AI algorithms for energy monitoring and control, manufacturers can reduce energy waste, lower operational costs, and minimize their environmental footprint.

Additionally, AI can enable predictive energy management by forecasting energy demand and dynamically adjusting energy usage to align with production schedules and demand fluctuations, ultimately contributing to sustainable and efficient manufacturing operations.

Inventory Management

Optimizing inventory management is essential for balancing supply and demand, minimizing carrying costs, and ensuring product availability. AI-powered inventory management systems can analyze historical sales data, market trends, and supply chain dynamics to optimize inventory levels and replenishment strategies.

Manufacturers can reduce excess inventory, prevent stockouts, and improve inventory turnover rates by leveraging AI for demand forecasting and inventory optimization. This leads to cost savings, improved cash flow, and enhanced responsiveness to customer demand.

Workforce Planning

AI-driven workforce planning tools can analyze production schedules, labor requirements, and skill sets to optimize workforce allocation and scheduling. By considering factors such as production targets, employee availability, and skill requirements, AI can help manufacturers achieve efficient workforce utilization and productivity.

Furthermore, AI can facilitate the identification of skill gaps and training needs, enabling manufacturers to develop and retain a skilled workforce capable of meeting evolving production demands and technological advancements.

Safety and Compliance

Ensuring safety and compliance with regulations is paramount in manufacturing operations. AI technologies offer capabilities to enhance risk assessment, regulatory compliance, and worker safety in manufacturing environments.

Risk Assessment

AI-based risk assessment systems can analyze operational data, environmental conditions, and historical incident records to identify potential safety hazards and risks in manufacturing processes. These systems can predict and mitigate risks by leveraging machine learning algorithms, ultimately contributing to a safer work environment.

Moreover, AI can enable real-time monitoring of safety-critical parameters and provide early warnings or interventions to prevent accidents and ensure workers' well-being.

Regulatory Compliance

Compliance with industry regulations and standards is essential for manufacturing operations. AI technologies can assist manufacturers in monitoring and ensuring compliance with regulatory requirements, such as environmental regulations, product safety standards, and workplace safety guidelines.

By leveraging AI for automated compliance monitoring and reporting, manufacturers can streamline regulatory adherence processes, reduce compliance-related risks, and demonstrate a commitment to ethical and responsible business practices.

Worker Safety

AI-driven technologies, such as predictive analytics and IoT-enabled safety systems, can enhance worker safety in manufacturing facilities. AI can identify potential safety hazards and provide real-time insights to prevent accidents and injuries by analyzing data from sensors, wearable devices, and environmental monitoring systems.

Furthermore, AI can support the development of safety training programs, ergonomic assessments, and proactive safety measures to create a culture of safety and well-being for the workforce.

Review Questions

1. Which of the following is a benefit of AI in manufacturing related to process optimization?

    A. Predictive Maintenance

    B. Quality Control

    C. Supply Chain Management

2. What is the benefit of AI in manufacturing related to product innovation?

    A. Customization and Personalization

    B. Smart Manufacturing

    C. Design Optimization

3. Which of the following is a benefit of AI in manufacturing related to resource management?

    A. Workforce Planning

    B. Energy Efficiency

    C. Inventory Management

4. what does the term 'safety and compliance' refer to in the context of AI in manufacturing?

    A. Worker Safety

B. Regulatory Compliance

C. Risk Assessment

5. Which of the following is not a benefit of AI in manufacturing?

   A. AI in Agriculture

   B. Smart Manufacturing

   C. Quality Control

CHAPTER 5

Benefits of AI in Schools

Personalized Learning

Personalized learning is a key benefit of integrating AI in schools. Adaptive learning platforms utilize AI algorithms to tailor educational content and pace to each student's needs. These platforms analyze students' learning patterns and performance to provide customized learning experiences. By adapting to students' strengths and weaknesses, adaptive learning platforms help optimize the learning process.

Individualized lesson plans are another aspect of personalized learning made possible by AI. With the help of AI-powered tools, teachers can create lesson plans that cater to each student's specific needs and learning styles. This level of customization ensures that students receive targeted instruction and support, leading to improved academic outcomes.

Student progress tracking is enhanced through AI systems that can analyze and interpret large volumes of data to provide insights into individual student performance. By identifying areas where students may be struggling or excelling, educators can intervene with targeted support and enrichment activities, ultimately fostering a more personalized and effective learning experience for each student.

Teacher Support and Development

AI in schools also benefits teachers by providing support in various aspects of their roles. Automated grading systems powered by AI can streamline the assessment process, allowing teachers to focus more on providing personalized feedback and support to their students. These systems can efficiently evaluate assignments, quizzes, and tests, saving teachers valuable time and effort.

AI-enhanced professional development tools offer educators opportunities for continuous growth and improvement. AI-powered platforms can recommend relevant resources, workshops, and training programs based on teachers' specific areas of interest and professional goals. This personalized approach to professional development helps teachers stay updated with the latest teaching methodologies and educational trends.

AI also aids in lesson plan generation by providing teachers with insights and suggestions for creating engaging and effective lesson plans. By analyzing student performance data and curriculum requirements, AI tools can recommend instructional strategies and content that align with students' learning needs and educational objectives.

Administrative Efficiency

AI contributes to school administrative efficiency by automating student enrollment and scheduling tasks. AI-powered systems can streamline enrollment by managing student data, processing applications, and ensuring accurate placement. Additionally, AI algorithms can optimize scheduling by considering student preferences, teacher availability, and resource allocation, resulting in more efficient and balanced timetables.

Resource allocation is another area where AI can significantly impact. By analyzing data on resource usage, student needs, and budget constraints, AI systems can provide insights and recommendations for optimizing resource allocation, ensuring that educational materials, facilities, and support services are distributed effectively to meet the needs of students and educators.

AI systems that automatically track and analyze student attendance data simplify and improve attendance monitoring. By identifying patterns and trends in attendance, schools can implement targeted interventions to support students with attendance challenges and ensure a safe and inclusive learning environment.

Special Education Support

AI plays a crucial role in supporting special education programs in schools. AI-powered customized learning plans enable educators to create individualized educational strategies for students with diverse learning needs. By leveraging AI tools to analyze students' strengths, challenges, and learning styles, educators can design personalized learning plans that cater to each student's unique requirements.

AI systems support behavioral analysis, which helps educators understand and address the behavioral dynamics of students in special education programs. By analyzing behavioral data, AI can provide insights into patterns and triggers, enabling educators to develop targeted interventions and support strategies to promote positive behavior and social-emotional development.

AI-powered tools can enhance speech and language therapy by providing personalized interventions and support for students with speech and language challenges. AI-based speech recognition and analysis tools can assist speech therapists in assessing students' speech patterns, providing targeted exercises, and tracking progress, ultimately improving the effectiveness of speech and language therapy programs.

Review Questions

1. Which of the following is a benefit of AI in schools related to personalized learning?

    A. Professional Development Tools

    B. Automated Grading

    C. Adaptive Learning Platforms

2. What is the benefit of AI in schools related to teacher support and development?

    A. Customized Learning Plans

    B. Student Enrollment and Scheduling

    C. Automated Grading

3. Which aspect of administrative efficiency in schools can be improved with AI?

    A. Resource Allocation

    B. Speech and Language Therapy

    C. Behavioral Analysis

4. In what way does AI support special education in schools?

    A. Professional Development Tools

    B. Adaptive Learning Platforms

    C. Customized Learning Plans

5. Which of the following is a benefit of AI in schools related to personalized learning?

    A. Student Progress Tracking

    B. Lesson Plan Generation

    C. Attendance Monitoring

CHAPTER 6

Benefits of AI for Writers

Content Creation and Curation

AI offers writers various tools and technologies to assist in content creation and curation. AI writing assistants are becoming increasingly popular among writers. These tools utilize natural language processing and machine learning algorithms to provide suggestions and corrections and even generate content based on the writer's input. They can help writers overcome writer's block, improve writing efficiency, and enhance the overall quality of their content.

Idea generation is another area where AI can benefit writers. AI-powered idea-generation tools can analyze trends, user behavior, and content performance to suggest relevant and engaging topics for writers to explore. By leveraging data-driven insights, writers can discover new angles and perspectives for their content, increasing reader engagement and relevance.

Content recommendation systems powered by AI can assist writers in identifying related or complementary content to enhance their work. These systems analyze the writer's content and audience preferences to suggest relevant articles, research papers, or multimedia resources that can enrich the writer's work and provide additional context or depth.

Language and Style Enhancement

AI tools designed for language and style enhancement offer writers advanced capabilities to refine their writing. AI-powered grammar and spelling correction tools can accurately identify and rectify grammatical errors, spelling mistakes, and punctuation issues. These tools provide writers with real-time feedback, enabling them to produce error-free and polished content.

Tone and voice analysis tools utilize AI to evaluate the emotional tone, style, and voice of writing. By analyzing language patterns and word choices, these tools can provide insights into the content's intended emotional impact. Writers can use this feedback to ensure that their writing aligns with the desired tone and resonates effectively with their target audience.

AI-powered translation and localization tools enable writers to reach a global audience by facilitating accurate and efficient content translation into multiple languages. These tools leverage natural language processing and machine translation algorithms to ensure that the essence and meaning of the content are preserved across different languages and cultural contexts.

Research and Fact-Checking

AI plays a crucial role in assisting writers with research and fact-checking processes. Information retrieval tools powered by AI can efficiently gather relevant data, statistics, and references from diverse sources, saving writers valuable time and effort in the research phase. These tools can aggregate and organize information, providing writers with comprehensive insights to support their content creation.

Plagiarism detection tools powered by AI are essential for writers to maintain originality and integrity in their work. These tools compare the writer's content with a vast database of existing publications and online sources to identify any instances of plagiarism. By detecting and highlighting potential plagiarism, writers can ensure the authenticity of their work and uphold ethical writing practices.

Data verification tools powered by AI enable writers to validate the accuracy and credibility of the information they incorporate into their content. These tools can cross-reference data points, verify sources, and identify inconsistencies, empowering writers to present well-researched and reliable information to their audience.

Workflow Optimization

AI offers writers various tools and platforms to optimize workflow and enhance productivity. AI-powered project management tools provide writers with features for task organization, scheduling, and progress tracking. These tools streamline project management processes, allowing writers to manage multiple writing projects efficiently, collaborate with team members, and meet deadlines effectively.

Collaborative writing platforms leverage AI to facilitate seamless collaboration among writers, editors, and other stakeholders involved in the content creation process. These platforms offer features for version control, real-time editing, and feedback integration, enabling teams to work together harmoniously and produce high-quality content collectively.

Deadline management tools powered by AI assist writers in prioritizing tasks, setting deadlines, and effectively managing their time. These tools can analyze the writer's workload, project timelines, and individual writing pace to provide personalized deadline recommendations and reminders, helping writers stay organized and focused on meeting their writing goals.

Review Questions

1. What are the benefits of AI for writers related to content creation and curation?

    A. Automated Writing Assistance

    B. Grammar and Spelling Correction

    C. Tone and Voice Analysis

2. Which aspect of AI for writers involves language and style enhancement?

    A. Grammar and Spelling Correction

    B. Idea Generation

    C. Plagiarism Detection

3. What does AI for writers help with in terms of research and fact-checking?

    A. Collaborative Writing Platforms

    B. Information Retrieval

    C. Project Management Tools

4. How does AI for writers contribute to workflow optimization?

    A. Automated Writing Assistance

    B. Project Management Tools

    C. Content Recommendation

5. Which AI benefit for writers involves translation and localization?

    A. Data Verification

    B. Tone and Voice Analysis

    C. Translation and Localization

CHAPTER 7

Common AI Programs

Machine Learning Frameworks

Machine learning frameworks are essential tools for developing and implementing machine learning models. These frameworks provide a set of libraries and tools that enable developers to build, train, and deploy machine learning algorithms efficiently. Here are some of the most widely used machine learning frameworks:

TensorFlow

TensorFlow is an open-source machine learning framework developed by the Google Brain team. It provides a comprehensive ecosystem of tools, libraries, and community resources for building and deploying machine learning models. TensorFlow supports a wide range of applications, including natural language processing, computer vision, and reinforcement learning.

One of TensorFlow's key features is its flexibility and scalability, which make it suitable for both research and production environments. It offers high-level APIs for quick model prototyping and lower-level APIs for fine-grained control over model architecture and training process.

With the introduction of TensorFlow 2.0, the framework has become more user-friendly and accessible. It incorporates eager execution for immediate model iteration and deployment. TensorFlow's extensive documentation and active community make it a popular choice for machine learning practitioners and researchers.

PyTorch

PyTorch is another popular open-source machine learning framework developed by Facebook's AI Research lab. It is known for its dynamic computation graph and intuitive programming interface, making it particularly favored by researchers and developers for its ease of use and flexibility.

PyTorch's dynamic computation graph allows for more dynamic model architectures and easier debugging, making it suitable for rapid prototyping and experimentation. It also provides a rich set of libraries for tasks such as image and text processing, reinforcement learning, and generative modeling.

One of PyTorch's critical advantages is its strong support for deep learning research. It focuses on providing tools for building and training complex neural network architectures. Its seamless integration with Python and active community contribute to its widespread adoption in the machine learning community.

Scikit-learn

Scikit-learn is a versatile and user-friendly machine-learning library built on top of NumPy, SciPy, and Matplotlib. It provides simple and efficient tools for data mining and data analysis, making it an ideal choice for beginners and experienced practitioners alike.

Scikit-learn offers a wide range of machine learning algorithms, including classification, regression, clustering, and dimensionality reduction. Its well-designed and consistent API makes it easy to experiment with different models and perform model evaluation and validation.

With its emphasis on usability and accessibility, Scikit-learn has become a go-to library for feature extraction, model selection, and hyperparameter tuning tasks. Its extensive documentation and active community support make it an essential tool for machine learning projects across various domains.

Natural Language Processing Tools

Natural language processing (NLP) tools are essential for processing and analyzing human language data, enabling language translation, sentiment analysis, and text generation applications. Here are some of the prominent NLP tools used in the industry:

NLTK (Natural Language Toolkit)

NLTK is a leading platform for building Python programs to work with human language data. It provides easy-to-use interfaces to over 50 corpora and lexical resources, along with a suite of text-processing libraries for classification, tokenization, stemming, tagging, parsing, and semantic reasoning.

One of the key strengths of NLTK is its extensive collection of resources and tools for teaching and research in NLP and corpus linguistics. It has been widely adopted in academia and industry for its comprehensive coverage of NLP tasks and its support for multiple languages.

With its rich set of documentation and tutorials, NLTK serves as an invaluable resource for NLP practitioners and researchers, offering a solid foundation for developing and deploying NLP applications.

SpaCy

SpaCy is a modern and efficient NLP library designed for production usage. It provides pre-trained models for various NLP tasks, including named entity recognition, part-of-speech tagging, dependency parsing, and text classification. SpaCy's focus on performance and usability makes it a popular choice for building scalable NLP pipelines.

One key advantage of SpaCy is its speed and memory efficiency, which allow for real-time processing of large volumes of text data. It also offers seamless integration with deep learning frameworks such as TensorFlow and PyTorch, enabling the development of end-to-end NLP solutions.

SpaCy's emphasis on developer experience and its support for multiple languages make it a valuable tool for building NLP applications across diverse domains, from information extraction and chatbots to content analysis and search engines.

Gensim

Gensim is a robust and efficient library for topic modeling and document similarity analysis. It provides tools for building unsupervised models such as Latent Semantic Analysis (LSA) and Latent Dirichlet Allocation (LDA) and word embedding models like Word2Vec and Doc2Vec.

One of the key strengths of Gensim is its focus on semantic analysis and document similarity, making it suitable for tasks such as document clustering, information retrieval, and recommendation systems. Its support for large-scale text corpora and its memory-efficient algorithms contribute to its popularity in the NLP community.

Gensim's user-friendly interfaces and extensive documentation make it an essential tool for researchers and practitioners working on text mining, information retrieval, and natural language understanding.

Computer Vision Software

Computer vision software plays a crucial role in analyzing and interpreting visual data, enabling applications such as image recognition, object detection, and video analysis. Here are some of the prominent computer vision software used in the industry:

OpenCV

OpenCV is a widely used open-source computer vision library that provides a comprehensive set of tools for image processing, feature detection, object recognition, and camera calibration. It offers various algorithms for tasks such as edge detection, image segmentation, and feature matching.

One key advantage of OpenCV is its cross-platform support and compatibility with multiple programming languages, including C++, Python, and Java. It also provides a rich collection of pre-trained models and datasets for rapidly developing computer vision applications.

OpenCV's active community and extensive documentation make it a go-to library for researchers and developers working on projects such as autonomous vehicles, augmented reality, and robotics.

Dlib

Dlib is a modern C++ toolkit for machine learning and computer vision applications. It offers a wide range of facial recognition, object detection, image alignment, and shape prediction tools. Dlib's focus on high-quality implementations and efficient algorithms makes it a popular choice for real-time computer vision tasks.

One of Dlib's key strengths is its support for deep learning models and integration with popular deep learning frameworks such as TensorFlow and PyTorch. It also provides tools for training custom object detectors and shape predictors, making it suitable for a wide range of computer vision applications.

Dlib's emphasis on performance and active developer community have contributed to its widespread adoption in the computer vision and machine learning communities.

SimpleCV

SimpleCV is an open-source framework for building computer vision applications with Python. It provides a high-level interface for image processing, feature extraction, and object tracking, making it suitable for rapid prototyping and experimentation in computer vision projects.

One key advantage of SimpleCV is its simplicity and ease of use. It allows both beginners and experienced developers to quickly build and test computer vision algorithms. It also integrates with popular hardware platforms such as Raspberry Pi and Arduino for embedded vision applications.

SimpleCV's focus on accessibility and its support for educational initiatives make it a valuable tool for teaching and learning computer vision concepts and applications.

Chatbot Platforms

Chatbot platforms are essential for building and deploying conversational agents to interact with users in natural language. These platforms provide tools for designing, training, and integrating chatbots into various applications. Here are some of the prominent chatbot platforms used in the industry:

Dialogflow

Dialogflow, formerly known as API.ai, is a powerful platform for building natural language understanding and conversational interfaces. It offers a rich set of tools for designing chatbot conversation flows, training language models, and integrating with messaging platforms and voice assistants.

One of Dialogflow's key strengths is its support for multi-platform deployment. This allows developers to create chatbots seamlessly interacting across web, mobile, and voice interfaces. Dialogflow also provides pre-built agents for common use cases such as customer support, e-commerce, and productivity.

Dialogflow's intuitive interface and extensive documentation make it a popular choice for developers and businesses looking to create engaging and intelligent conversational experiences.

IBM Watson Assistant

IBM Watson Assistant is a robust platform for building AI-powered chatbots and virtual agents. It provides tools for natural language understanding, intent recognition, and context management, enabling developers to create sophisticated conversational interfaces for various applications.

One key advantage of IBM Watson Assistant is its integration with IBM's AI services and cloud infrastructure, which allows for seamless deployment and scaling of chatbot applications. It also offers advanced features such as sentiment analysis, entity extraction, and multi-language support.

IBM Watson Assistant's enterprise-grade capabilities and its focus on security and compliance make it a preferred choice for businesses and organizations seeking to deploy AI-driven chatbot solutions.

Microsoft Bot Framework

Microsoft Bot Framework is a comprehensive platform for building, connecting, testing, and deploying intelligent bots. It provides a wide range of tools for developing conversational agents that can interact across multiple channels, including web, mobile, and messaging platforms.

One of Microsoft Bot Framework's key strengths is its integration with Azure services. This enables developers to leverage cloud-based AI capabilities for natural language processing, speech recognition, and language understanding. It also offers support for rich media and adaptive cards for creating visually engaging chatbot experiences.

Microsoft Bot Framework's extensive documentation, SDKs, and community support make it a valuable resource for developers and organizations looking to create AI-powered chatbots for customer engagement and support.

Review Questions

1. Which of the following is a machine learning framework?

   A. SpaCy

   B. TensorFlow

   C. NLTK

2. Which of the following is a natural language processing tool?

   A. OpenCV

   B. Dlib

   C. NLTK (Natural Language Toolkit)

3. Which of the following is a computer vision software?

   A. PyTorch

   B. OpenCV

   C. Dialogflow

4. Which of the following is a chatbot platform?

   A. Dialogflow

   B. Gensim

   C. Scikit-learn

5. Which of the following is not a machine learning framework?

   A. PyTorch

   B. Microsoft Bot Framework

   C. Scikit-learn

CHAPTER 8

AI Terminology and Languages

Key AI Terminology

Artificial Neural Network: An artificial neural network (ANN) is a computational model inspired by the structure and functions of biological neural networks in the human brain. It consists of interconnected nodes, called neurons, which work together to process and analyze complex data patterns. ANNs are commonly used in machine learning to recognize patterns, make predictions, and solve complex problems.

Supervised Learning: Supervised learning is a type of machine learning where the model is trained on a labeled dataset, meaning the input data is paired with the correct output. The algorithm learns to make predictions by finding patterns in the input-output pairs. It is commonly used in tasks such as classification, regression, and prediction.

Unsupervised Learning: Unsupervised learning is a type of machine learning where the model is trained on an unlabeled dataset, and it learns to find patterns and structures in the data without explicit guidance. It is commonly used in clustering, dimensionality reduction, and anomaly detection tasks.

Programming Languages for AI

Python: Python is a high-level, general-purpose programming language known for its simplicity and readability. It has a rich ecosystem of libraries and frameworks for machine learning, such as TensorFlow, PyTorch, and scikit-learn. Python's versatility and ease of use make it a popular choice for AI development.

R: R is a programming language and environment specifically designed for statistical computing and graphics. It provides a wide range of statistical and graphical techniques, making it well-suited for data analysis and visualization in AI applications. R's extensive libraries and packages make it a preferred language for statistical modeling and data analysis.

Java: Java is a widely-used, object-oriented programming language known for its platform independence and robustness. While not as commonly associated with AI as Python or R, Java is used in AI development for its performance, scalability, and enterprise-level applications. It is often employed in building AI applications for large-scale systems and business solutions.

AI Development Tools

Jupyter Notebooks: Jupyter Notebooks is an open-source web application that allows users to create and share documents containing live code, equations, visualizations, and narrative text. It is widely used in AI development for interactive data exploration, visualization, and collaborative coding. Jupyter Notebooks support various programming languages, including Python, R, and Julia.

Google Colab: Google Colab is a cloud-based platform provided by Google that allows users to write and execute Python code in a collaborative environment. It provides free access to GPU and TPU for accelerating machine learning tasks. Google Colab is popular for its ease of use, integration with Google Drive, and the ability to run heavy AI workloads in the cloud.

Spyder: Spyder is an open-source integrated development environment (IDE) designed for scientific computing, data analysis, and AI development. It provides a powerful code editor, interactive console, and variable explorer, making it suitable for prototyping and debugging AI applications. Spyder's integration with popular libraries like NumPy and pandas makes it a preferred choice for data-centric AI projects.

Ethical AI Principles

Fairness and Bias: Fairness and bias in AI refer to the ethical considerations around ensuring that AI systems and algorithms do not discriminate against individuals or groups based on protected attributes such as race, gender, or age. Addressing fairness and bias involves designing AI systems that are equitable and unbiased in their decision-making processes.

Transparency: Transparency in AI pertains to the visibility and understandability of AI systems and their decision-making processes. It involves making AI algorithms and models interpretable and explainable to users and stakeholders, thereby fostering trust and accountability in AI applications.

Accountability: Accountability in AI involves holding individuals, organizations, and AI systems responsible for the outcomes and impacts of AI applications. It encompasses establishing mechanisms for oversight, redressal, and ethical governance to ensure that AI technologies are used responsibly and ethically.

Review Questions

1. What is the term for a computational model inspired by the structure and function of the human brain?

   A. Unsupervised Learning

   B. Artificial Neural Network

   C. Supervised Learning

2. Which of the following is a programming language commonly used for AI development?

   A. Java

   B. Python

   C. R

3. Which of the following is a popular AI development tool that provides an interactive environment for writing and running code?

   A. Jupyter Notebooks

   B. Google Colab

C. Spyder

4. What ethical principle in AI focuses on ensuring that AI systems do not exhibit bias or discrimination?

    A. Fairness and Bias

    B. Transparency

    C. Accountability

5. What type of learning involves training a model on labeled data with known input-output pairs?

    A. Supervised Learning

    B. Unsupervised Learning

    C. Artificial Neural Network

CHAPTER 9

Using Common AI Programs

Machine Learning Applications

Machine learning applications have become increasingly prevalent in various industries, offering advanced capabilities for data analysis and prediction. The following are some common applications of machine learning:

Predictive Analytics

Predictive analytics leverages machine learning algorithms to forecast future outcomes based on historical data. Organizations use predictive analytics to anticipate trends, identify potential risks, and make informed decisions. For example, in finance, predictive analytics is utilized for credit scoring to assess the likelihood of loan default, while in marketing, it is employed to forecast customer behavior and preferences.

One of the key advantages of predictive analytics is its ability to uncover patterns and correlations within large datasets, enabling businesses to optimize their strategies and mitigate potential risks. By harnessing the power of machine learning, predictive analytics empowers organizations to make proactive and data-driven decisions.

Image Recognition

Image recognition, also known as computer vision, is a machine learning application that enables computers to interpret and understand visual information from images and videos. This technology has diverse applications, ranging from facial recognition for security purposes to medical image analysis for diagnosing diseases.

In the healthcare industry, image recognition algorithms are employed to analyze medical images such as X-rays, MRIs, and CT scans, assisting healthcare professionals in detecting abnormalities and making accurate diagnoses. Moreover, in the retail sector, image recognition is utilized for visual search capabilities, allowing consumers to search for products using images rather than keywords.

Recommendation Systems

Recommendation systems utilize machine learning algorithms to provide personalized suggestions to users based on their preferences and behavior. These systems are widely used in e-commerce platforms, streaming services, and content websites to enhance user experience and engagement.

For instance, e-commerce companies leverage recommendation systems to offer personalized product recommendations, thereby increasing sales and customer satisfaction. Similarly, streaming services use these systems to suggest movies, TV shows, or music based on users' viewing or listening history, ultimately improving user retention and engagement.

Natural Language Processing Applications

Natural language processing (NLP) applications enable machines to understand, interpret, and generate human language, leading to a wide array of practical uses. The following are some common applications of NLP:

Sentiment Analysis

Sentiment analysis, also known as opinion mining, involves the use of NLP techniques to determine the sentiment expressed in a piece of text, such as positive, negative, or neutral. This application is widely employed in social media monitoring, customer feedback analysis, and market research to gauge public opinion and sentiment towards products, services, or brands.

By analyzing and categorizing textual data, sentiment analysis provides valuable insights for businesses to understand customer perceptions, identify emerging trends, and tailor their strategies to meet consumer expectations.

Text Generation

Text generation applications utilize NLP models, such as recurrent neural networks and transformer-based architectures, to generate human-like text based on given prompts or contexts. These models have demonstrated remarkable capabilities in producing coherent and contextually relevant text, enabling applications in content generation, chatbots, and language translation.

For instance, text generation models are utilized in chatbot development to provide natural and engaging conversational experiences for users. Additionally, they are employed in language translation services to generate accurate and fluent translations of text from one language to another.

Language Translation

Language translation applications leverage NLP techniques to translate text or speech from one language to another, facilitating cross-lingual communication and information access. With the advancements in machine translation models, such as neural machine translation, the quality and accuracy of language translation have significantly improved.

These applications have profound implications for global business, cross-cultural communication, and accessibility to information across different linguistic communities. Language translation technologies play a pivotal role in breaking down language barriers and fostering international collaboration and understanding.

Computer Vision Applications

Computer vision applications encompass a broad spectrum of uses, from object detection and recognition to medical imaging analysis. The following are some common applications of computer vision:

Object Detection

Object detection is a computer vision application that involves identifying and locating objects within images or videos. This technology has diverse applications, including autonomous vehicles, surveillance systems, and industrial automation.

In the context of autonomous vehicles, object detection algorithms enable vehicles to perceive and recognize pedestrians, vehicles, and road signs, contributing to the safety and reliability of self-driving systems. Similarly, in retail and manufacturing, object detection is utilized for inventory management, quality control, and product recognition.

Facial Recognition

Facial recognition technology utilizes computer vision algorithms to identify and verify individuals based on their facial features. This application has found widespread use in security systems, access control, and law enforcement for identifying persons of interest and enhancing public safety.

Moreover, facial recognition has been integrated into consumer devices, such as smartphones and laptops, for biometric authentication and personalized user experiences. However, ethical considerations and privacy concerns surrounding facial recognition have sparked debates regarding its responsible and transparent deployment.

Medical Imaging Analysis

Medical imaging analysis applications harness computer vision techniques to interpret and analyze medical images, including X-rays, CT scans, and histopathology slides. These applications aid healthcare professionals in diagnosing diseases, planning treatments, and monitoring patient health.

By leveraging machine learning algorithms, medical imaging analysis can assist in early detection of abnormalities, quantification of disease progression, and identification of potential treatment responses. The integration of computer vision in healthcare has the potential to revolutionize medical diagnostics and improve patient outcomes.

Chatbot Applications

Chatbots, powered by AI and natural language processing, are utilized in various domains to automate conversations and provide interactive assistance to users. The following are some common applications of chatbots:

Customer Support

Chatbots are extensively used in customer support services to handle inquiries, provide information, and assist users with troubleshooting. By leveraging AI algorithms, chatbots can understand user queries, offer relevant solutions, and escalate complex issues to human agents when necessary.

Organizations deploy customer support chatbots to enhance response times, streamline customer interactions, and deliver consistent support experiences across multiple communication channels, including websites, messaging platforms, and mobile applications.

Virtual Assistants

Virtual assistants, also known as intelligent personal assistants, are AI-powered chatbots designed to perform tasks and provide information based on user commands or requests. These assistants are integrated into devices and applications to offer personalized and context-aware assistance to users.

Virtual assistants can perform a wide range of functions, including setting reminders, managing schedules, retrieving information, and controlling smart home devices. With advancements in natural language understanding and dialogue management, virtual assistants are evolving to become indispensable tools for productivity and convenience.

Educational Chatbots

Educational chatbots are designed to support learning and provide educational content, guidance, and assessment to students. These chatbots can offer personalized tutoring, answer academic queries, and facilitate interactive learning experiences through conversational interactions.

By leveraging AI and natural language processing, educational chatbots aim to enhance student engagement, provide instant feedback, and adapt to individual learning needs. These applications have the potential to revolutionize the education landscape by offering personalized and accessible learning experiences.

Review Questions

1. Which of the following is an example of a machine learning application?

    A. Language Translation

    B. Predictive Analytics

    C. Facial Recognition

2. What is an example of a natural language processing application?

    A. Sentiment Analysis

    B. Object Detection

    C. Medical Imaging Analysis

3. Which of the following is a computer vision application?

    A. Customer Support

B. Facial Recognition

C. Virtual Assistants

4. In which of the following chatbot applications would a chatbot be used for answering customer queries?

    A. Educational Chatbots

    B. Customer Support

    C. Virtual Assistants

5. What type of application involves generating text based on input?

    A. Text Generation

    B. Recommendation Systems

    C. Image Recognition

CHAPTER 10

Introduction to AI-Simulated Chatbots

Understanding Chatbots

Chatbots, also known as conversational agents or virtual assistants, are AI-powered programs designed to simulate human conversation. Their primary purpose is to interact with users in a natural language format, providing information, answering questions, and assisting with various tasks. Chatbots can be integrated into messaging platforms, websites, and voice assistants, offering a seamless and efficient way to engage with users.

There are different types of chatbots, each serving specific purposes based on their design and functionality. Understanding the definition, purpose, and types of chatbots is essential for leveraging their capabilities in various domains.

Definition and Purpose

The definition of a chatbot encompasses its ability to understand and respond to natural language input from users. It acts as a virtual conversational partner, capable of interpreting queries, providing relevant information, and executing tasks based on user interactions. The purpose of chatbots varies across industries and applications, ranging from customer support and sales assistance to information retrieval and task automation.

Chatbots are designed to streamline communication processes, enhance user experiences, and provide efficient solutions to common queries and tasks. They serve as an accessible and interactive interface for users to engage with digital systems and services.

Types of Chatbots

Chatbots can be categorized into different types based on their functionality and capabilities. The main types of chatbots include rule-based chatbots, AI-powered chatbots, and hybrid chatbots. Rule-based chatbots operate on predefined rules and patterns, while AI-powered chatbots leverage machine learning and natural language processing to understand and respond to user input. Hybrid chatbots combine elements of both rule-based and AI-powered approaches to offer a balanced conversational experience.

Additionally, chatbots can be classified based on their deployment, such as website chatbots, messaging app chatbots, and voice assistant chatbots. Each type serves specific communication channels and user interaction contexts, catering to diverse user preferences and needs.

How Chatbots Work

Chatbots work through a combination of natural language processing (NLP), machine learning algorithms, and predefined conversational flows. When a user interacts with a chatbot by sending a message or input, the chatbot processes the text, identifies the user's intent, and generates an appropriate response. This process involves parsing and understanding the user's input, retrieving relevant information or performing actions, and formulating a natural language response to communicate with the user.

Behind the scenes, chatbots utilize NLP models to comprehend user messages, entity recognition to extract key information, and dialogue management to maintain context and coherence in conversations. AI-powered chatbots continuously learn from user interactions and feedback, improving their conversational abilities and expanding their knowledge base over time.

Chatbot Development Platforms

Chatbot development platforms provide the necessary tools and frameworks to create, deploy, and manage chatbots across different communication channels. These platforms offer a range of features, including natural language understanding, conversation design, integration capabilities, and analytics to empower developers and organizations in building effective chatbot solutions.

The following are prominent chatbot development platforms widely used for creating AI simulated chatbots:

Dialogflow

Dialogflow, a product by Google, is a comprehensive development platform for building conversational interfaces, including chatbots and voice applications. It offers natural language understanding, context management, and integration with various messaging platforms and voice assistants. Dialogflow's rich set of features and easy integration with Google Cloud services make it a popular choice for developing AI chatbots.

Developers can leverage Dialogflow's pre-built agents, entity recognition, and intent mapping to create conversational experiences tailored to specific use cases, such as customer support, information retrieval, and task automation.

IBM Watson Assistant

IBM Watson Assistant is an AI-powered chatbot development platform that enables organizations to design and deploy conversational solutions across multiple channels. It offers advanced natural language processing capabilities, intent recognition, and entity extraction to understand user input and provide accurate responses.

IBM Watson Assistant also provides integration with third-party systems and services, allowing developers to create seamless conversational experiences for users.

With its cognitive computing capabilities, IBM Watson Assistant empowers developers to build chatbots that can handle complex queries, personalize interactions, and adapt to user preferences over time.

Microsoft Bot Framework

The Microsoft Bot Framework is a comprehensive platform for building, connecting, testing, and deploying chatbots across various channels, including websites, messaging platforms, and voice interfaces. It offers a range of development tools, SDKs, and services to create intelligent and interactive chatbot experiences. The framework supports natural language understanding, dialog management, and integration with Microsoft Azure services for scalable and reliable chatbot deployment.

Developers can leverage the Microsoft Bot Framework to create chatbots with rich multimedia support, adaptive card layouts, and multi-turn conversations, enhancing user engagement and interaction capabilities.

Chatbot Design and User Experience

Designing chatbots with a focus on conversational design, user interaction, and personalized experiences is crucial for creating engaging and effective AI simulated chatbots. The design and user experience aspects of chatbots encompass the conversational flow, user feedback mechanisms, and contextual understanding to deliver seamless and intuitive interactions.

Conversational Design

Conversational design involves structuring the flow of interactions between the chatbot and the user to ensure a natural and coherent conversation. It encompasses defining conversation paths, handling user inputs, and managing context to guide users through meaningful and productive interactions. Effective conversational design considers user intents, prompts for information, and clear communication of the chatbot's capabilities and limitations.

By focusing on conversational design, developers can create chatbots that engage users in meaningful dialogues, provide relevant information, and guide users towards accomplishing their goals effectively.

User Interaction and Feedback

User interaction and feedback mechanisms play a vital role in enhancing the overall user experience with chatbots. Providing clear prompts, acknowledging user input, and offering feedback on actions taken by the chatbot contribute to a more engaging and satisfying interaction. Additionally, incorporating user feedback loops and sentiment analysis enables chatbots to adapt to user preferences and continuously improve their conversational abilities.

Effective user interaction and feedback mechanisms foster a sense of understanding and responsiveness in chatbot interactions, leading to higher user satisfaction and engagement.

Personalization and Context

Personalization and context awareness are essential elements of chatbot design to create tailored and relevant experiences for users. By understanding user preferences, history of interactions, and contextual information, chatbots can deliver personalized responses, recommendations, and actions. Contextual awareness enables chatbots to maintain coherence in conversations, remember previous interactions, and adapt their responses based on the ongoing dialogue.

Incorporating personalization and context awareness in chatbot design enhances user engagement, fosters a sense of familiarity, and increases the effectiveness of chatbot interactions in addressing user needs.

Chatbot Integration

Chatbot integration involves deploying chatbots across different platforms and communication channels to reach and engage users effectively. Integrating chatbots with websites, messaging platforms, and voice assistants expands their accessibility and utility, enabling seamless interactions and user assistance.

Integration with Websites

Integrating chatbots with websites allows organizations to offer instant assistance, information retrieval, and interactive experiences to website visitors. Chatbots can be embedded as chat widgets, pop-up assistants, or dedicated chat pages, providing users with real-time support, personalized recommendations, and streamlined access to services and information.

Website integration empowers chatbots to serve as virtual assistants, guiding users through website navigation, answering queries, and facilitating transactions or interactions within the website environment.

Integration with Messaging Platforms

Messaging platforms, such as Facebook Messenger, WhatsApp, and Slack, serve as popular communication channels for users to engage with businesses, services, and brands. Integrating chatbots with messaging platforms enables organizations to offer automated customer support, transactional interactions, and personalized messaging experiences to users within their preferred messaging apps.

Chatbot integration with messaging platforms streamlines user engagement, facilitates seamless communication, and provides a convenient channel for users to access information and services.

Integration with Voice Assistants

Voice assistants, including Amazon Alexa, Google Assistant, and Apple Siri, present an opportunity for chatbots to extend their reach and functionality through voice interactions. Integrating chatbots with voice assistants enables users to access information, perform tasks, and engage in conversations using voice commands, expanding the accessibility and usability of chatbot solutions.

Voice assistant integration empowers chatbots to offer hands-free interactions, personalized voice responses, and seamless access to services and information through natural language voice commands.

Review Questions

1. What is the purpose of chatbots?

    A. To analyze data

    B. To create visual designs

    C. To automate repetitive tasks

    D. To provide entertainment

2. Which of the following is a chatbot development platform?

    A. Adobe Photoshop

    B. AutoCAD

    C. Dialogflow

    D. Microsoft Excel

3. What is conversational design in chatbots focused on?

    A. Creating visually appealing interfaces

    B. Optimizing website performance

    C. Designing natural and engaging conversations

    D. Developing complex algorithms

4. How can chatbots be integrated with messaging platforms?

    A. By creating interactive videos

B. By integrating with APIs of messaging platforms

C. By using QR codes

D. By embedding 3D models

5. What is the purpose of integrating chatbots with voice assistants?

A. To analyze user behavior

B. To improve website navigation

C. To create virtual reality experiences

D. To enable voice-based interactions with chatbots

CHAPTER 11

Building Simulated Chatbots Online

Online Chatbot Development Platforms

Online chatbot development platforms provide a user-friendly environment for creating and deploying chatbots without the need for extensive programming knowledge. These platforms offer a range of tools and features to design, build, and manage chatbots for various purposes. In this section, we will explore three popular online chatbot development platforms: Chatfuel, ManyChat, and Botsify.

Chatfuel

Chatfuel is a leading chatbot development platform that allows users to create AI chatbots for Facebook Messenger and other messaging platforms. It offers a visual interface and a drag-and-drop bot builder, making it easy for both beginners and experienced developers to design and deploy chatbots. Chatfuel provides a variety of templates, plugins, and integrations to enhance the functionality of chatbots, including e-commerce, lead generation, customer support, and more.

ManyChat

ManyChat is another popular platform for building chatbots on Facebook Messenger. It offers a user-friendly interface and a powerful visual bot builder that enables users to create interactive chatbot experiences without writing a single line of code. ManyChat provides features such as automated sequences, audience segmentation, and growth tools to help businesses engage with their audience and automate customer interactions through chatbots.

Botsify

Botsify is an AI chatbot platform that allows users to create chatbots for websites, Facebook Messenger, and other messaging channels. It offers a no-code chatbot builder with advanced features such as natural language understanding, multilingual support, and integration with third-party services. Botsify's drag-and-drop interface and pre-built templates make it easy for businesses to deploy chatbots for customer service, lead generation, and sales automation.

Creating a Basic Chatbot

Creating a basic chatbot involves several key steps, from setting up an account on a chatbot development platform to designing conversation flows and adding responses and actions. In this section, we will explore the fundamental process of creating a basic chatbot using online chatbot development platforms.

Setting Up an Account

Before creating a chatbot, users need to sign up and create an account on their chosen chatbot development platform. This typically involves providing basic information, such as email address, username, and password. Once the account is set up, users can access the platform's dashboard and begin building their chatbot.

Designing Conversation Flows

Designing conversation flows is a crucial aspect of creating a chatbot. It involves mapping out the various paths and interactions that the chatbot will have with users. This can be done using a visual flowchart or a drag-and-drop interface provided by the chatbot development platform. Conversation flows define how the chatbot responds to user inputs and guides the conversation towards achieving specific goals.

Adding Responses and Actions

Once the conversation flows are designed, users can add responses and actions to the chatbot. Responses include text, images, buttons, and other interactive elements that the chatbot can use to engage with users. Actions enable the chatbot to perform tasks such as sending messages, collecting user input, and integrating with external services or APIs to retrieve or store information.

Advanced Chatbot Features

Advanced chatbot features go beyond basic conversation flows and responses, offering more sophisticated capabilities to enhance the chatbot's functionality and user experience. In this section, we will explore three advanced features commonly found in online chatbot development platforms: natural language understanding, integration with APIs, and analytics and reporting.

Natural Language Understanding

Natural language understanding (NLU) allows chatbots to comprehend and interpret the meaning behind user messages, enabling more human-like and contextually relevant interactions. Advanced chatbot platforms provide NLU capabilities through machine learning models that can analyze and process natural language inputs, extract entities, and understand user intents to deliver accurate and personalized responses.

Integration with APIs

Integration with application programming interfaces (APIs) enables chatbots to access external data sources, services, and functionalities to enrich their capabilities. Chatbot development platforms offer integrations with popular APIs for tasks such as retrieving weather information, accessing databases, processing payments, and connecting with third-party applications to provide users with comprehensive and seamless experiences.

Analytics and Reporting

Analytics and reporting features provide valuable insights into the performance and effectiveness of chatbots. These features allow users to track user interactions, measure engagement metrics, analyze conversation trends, and gather feedback to continuously improve and optimize the chatbot's behavior. Chatbot platforms offer built-in analytics dashboards and reporting tools to monitor and evaluate chatbot performance.

Deploying and Testing Chatbots

Deploying and testing chatbots is a critical phase in the chatbot development process, ensuring that the chatbot functions as intended and delivers a seamless user experience. In this section, we will explore the steps involved in testing chatbots in a development environment, deploying them to websites, and gathering user feedback through testing.

Testing in Development Environment

Before deploying a chatbot to a live environment, it is essential to thoroughly test its functionality in a development environment. Chatbot development platforms provide testing tools and simulators that allow users to interact with the chatbot, simulate user inputs, and identify any issues or errors in the chatbot's behavior. Testing helps ensure that the chatbot is ready for deployment and can effectively handle user interactions.

Deploying to Websites

Once a chatbot is tested and refined, it can be deployed to websites and other digital platforms to engage with users. Chatbot development platforms offer integration options and plugins to seamlessly embed chatbots into websites, social media pages, and messaging channels. Deploying chatbots to websites involves configuring settings, generating embeddable code, and customizing the chatbot's appearance and behavior to align with the website's design and functionality.

User Testing and Feedback

After deploying a chatbot, it is important to gather user feedback and conduct user testing to assess the chatbot's performance in a real-world context. Chatbot platforms provide tools for collecting user feedback, analyzing user interactions, and monitoring chatbot usage patterns. User testing helps identify areas for improvement, gather insights for enhancing the chatbot's capabilities, and ensure that the chatbot meets user expectations.

Review Questions

1. Which of the following is an online chatbot development platform?

    A. Chatfuel

    B. Python

C. JavaScript

2. What is the process of designing conversation flows in chatbot development?

    A. Adding Responses and Actions

    B. Designing Conversation Flows

    C. Setting Up an Account

3. Which of the following is an advanced chatbot feature?

    A. Deploying to Websites

    B. Natural Language Understanding

    C. Setting Up an Account

4. What is the final step in chatbot development before deployment?

    A. Setting Up an Account

    B. Testing in Development Environment

    C. User Testing and Feedback

5. Which of the following platforms is used for deploying chatbots to websites?

    A. Botsify

    B. All of the above

    C. ManyChat

    D. Chatfuel

CHAPTER 12

AI Projects for High School Students

Introduction to AI Project Ideas

Undertaking an AI project can be an exciting and rewarding experience for high school students. It provides an opportunity to explore the fascinating world of artificial intelligence while developing valuable technical and problem-solving skills. Here are three engaging AI project ideas that high school students can consider:

Creating a Personalized Recommender System

A personalized recommender system is a software application that analyzes user preferences and behavior to provide personalized recommendations. High school students can develop a recommender system for a specific domain, such as movies, books, music, or online courses. The project involves understanding user data, implementing recommendation algorithms, and creating an intuitive user interface for displaying recommendations.

Students can explore collaborative filtering, content-based filtering, and hybrid recommendation techniques to enhance the accuracy and relevance of their recommender system. They can also incorporate user feedback and rating mechanisms to improve the system's performance over time.

Designing a Basic Chatbot

Designing a basic chatbot is an engaging AI project that allows students to delve into natural language processing and conversational AI. High school students can create a chatbot that simulates human-like conversation and provides helpful responses to user queries. The project involves designing conversation flows, implementing natural language understanding, and integrating the chatbot with messaging platforms or websites.

Students can explore different chatbot development platforms and frameworks to build their chatbot, and they can incorporate machine learning models for language understanding and context-aware responses. They can also experiment with sentiment analysis and user interaction to enhance the chatbot's conversational capabilities.

Building an Image Recognition App

Building an image recognition app is an exciting AI project that involves developing a system capable of identifying and classifying objects within images. High school students can explore deep learning and computer vision techniques to create an app that can recognize common objects, animals, or even handwritten digits. The project involves training image recognition models, integrating them into a user-friendly application, and testing the app's accuracy and performance.

Students can experiment with popular deep learning frameworks such as TensorFlow or PyTorch to train their image recognition models. They can also explore pre-trained models and transfer learning to leverage existing neural network architectures for their app development.

Tools and Resources for AI Projects

Undertaking an AI project requires access to the right tools and resources to support the development and implementation process. High school students can leverage various programming languages, AI development platforms, and online learning resources to enhance their project experience. Here are essential tools and resources for AI projects:

Programming Languages

High school students can choose from a range of programming languages to implement their AI projects. Python, with its rich libraries for machine learning and data analysis, is a popular choice for AI development. Its simplicity and readability make it an ideal language for students to learn and apply AI concepts. Additionally, R and Java are also widely used in AI for statistical analysis, data manipulation, and building AI applications.

Students can explore the syntax, libraries, and frameworks associated with these languages to determine the best fit for their project requirements. They can also engage in coding exercises and projects to strengthen their programming skills in the context of AI development.

AI Development Platforms

AI development platforms provide high school students with the necessary tools and environments to build and deploy AI applications. Platforms such as Jupyter Notebooks, Google Colab, and Spyder offer integrated development environments (IDEs) with support for data analysis, machine learning, and deep learning. These platforms enable students to write and execute code, visualize data, and collaborate on AI projects.

Students can explore the features and capabilities of these platforms to familiarize themselves with AI development workflows. They can also access tutorials and documentation to learn about the various tools and libraries available within these platforms.

Online Learning Resources

High school students can benefit from a wealth of online learning resources that provide tutorials, courses, and educational materials related to AI and machine learning. Platforms such as Coursera, Udemy, and Khan Academy offer a diverse range of AI-related courses, covering topics from introductory concepts to advanced algorithms and applications.

Students can leverage these resources to deepen their understanding of AI principles, explore specific AI techniques, and gain hands-on experience through practical exercises and projects. They can also participate in online communities and forums to seek guidance and support from experts and peers in the field of AI.

Guidance and Mentorship

Embarking on an AI project as a high school student can be an enriching experience, especially with the guidance and mentorship of educators, AI professionals, and supportive communities. Seeking support and mentorship can provide valuable insights, resources, and encouragement throughout the project journey. Here are avenues for seeking guidance and mentorship:

Seeking Support from Teachers

High school students can seek guidance and support from their teachers, particularly those with expertise in computer science, mathematics, or AI-related fields. Teachers can provide valuable insights, resources, and feedback to help students navigate the complexities of AI projects. They can also offer mentorship and assistance in understanding AI concepts, selecting project ideas, and refining project implementation.

Engaging with AI Communities

Participating in AI communities and forums allows high school students to connect with like-minded individuals, AI enthusiasts, and professionals in the field. Online platforms such as Stack Overflow, Reddit, and AI-specific forums provide opportunities to ask questions, share insights, and seek advice on AI project development. Engaging with these communities can offer diverse perspectives and valuable support for students' AI endeavors.

Connecting with Industry Professionals

High school students can explore opportunities to connect with industry professionals and experts in AI through networking events, workshops, and mentorship programs. Engaging with professionals in the AI industry can provide students with real-world insights, career guidance, and mentorship for their AI projects. Industry professionals can offer valuable feedback, share practical experiences, and inspire students to pursue their interests in AI.

Project Implementation and Presentation

Successfully implementing an AI project involves careful planning, execution, documentation, and presentation of the project outcomes. High school students can follow structured approaches to manage their project development and showcase their achievements effectively. Here are key aspects of project implementation and presentation:

Planning and Execution

Planning the AI project involves defining project goals, outlining project requirements, and creating a project timeline. High school students can break down their project into manageable tasks, set milestones, and allocate time for research, development, and testing. Effective project execution involves adhering to the project plan, managing resources, and adapting to unforeseen challenges during the development process.

Documentation and Reflection

Thorough documentation of the AI project is essential for capturing the project's journey, methodologies, and outcomes. High school students can maintain detailed records of their project activities, including code snippets, experimental results, and design decisions. Reflecting on the project's progress and challenges allows students to gain insights into their learning experiences and identify areas for improvement.

Showcasing the Project

Presenting the AI project showcases students' creativity, technical skills, and problem-solving abilities. High school students can prepare presentations, demonstrations, or project reports to communicate their project's objectives, methodologies, and results. Showcasing the project to peers, educators, and potential mentors provides an opportunity to receive feedback, recognition, and encouragement for their AI endeavors.

Review Questions

1. What are some AI project ideas for high school students?

    A. Designing a Basic Chatbot

    B. Developing a Weather Prediction Model

    C. Creating a Personalized Recommender System

    D. Building a Social Media Platform

2. Which of the following is a tool or resource for AI projects?

    A. Artistic Techniques

    B. Historical Documents

C. Mathematical Theorems

D. Programming Languages

3. How can high school students seek guidance and mentorship for their AI projects?

    A. Seeking Support from Teachers

    B. Attending Music Concerts

    C. Visiting Art Galleries

    D. Engaging with AI Communities

4. What is an important step in the project implementation and presentation process for high school students?

    A. Planning and Execution

    B. Singing a Song

    C. Playing Video Games

    D. Writing Poetry

5. Which of the following is NOT a part of project implementation and presentation for high school students?

    A. Planning and Execution

    B. Building a Time Machine

    C. Showcasing the Project

    D. Documentation and Reflection

CHAPTER 13

AI in Everyday Life

AI in Personal Devices

AI has become an integral part of personal devices, enhancing the user experience and providing advanced functionalities. Smartphones and virtual assistants are among the most prominent examples of AI integration in personal devices.

Smartphones and Virtual Assistants

Smartphones have evolved to incorporate AI-powered features that enable users to perform tasks more efficiently and intuitively. Virtual assistants such as Siri, Google Assistant, and Bixby utilize AI algorithms to understand and respond to user commands, provide personalized recommendations, and perform various tasks through voice interactions.

AI in smartphones also facilitates predictive text input, image recognition for photo organization, and context-aware suggestions based on user behavior and preferences. The integration of AI in personal devices has significantly transformed the way individuals interact with technology on a daily basis.

Smart Home Devices

The proliferation of smart home devices, including smart speakers, thermostats, and security systems, has been driven by AI advancements. These devices leverage AI to learn user habits, automate routine tasks, and adapt to changing environmental conditions. For instance, AI-powered smart home assistants can manage household appliances, adjust lighting based on occupancy, and provide real-time updates on weather and traffic.

Furthermore, AI enables seamless integration between different smart devices, allowing users to create interconnected and automated home environments that enhance convenience and energy efficiency.

Wearable Technology

Wearable technology, such as smartwatches and fitness trackers, harnesses AI to track and analyze various aspects of an individual's health and activity. These devices utilize AI algorithms to monitor heart rate, sleep patterns, and physical exercise, providing users with valuable insights into their well-being and fitness levels.

Moreover, AI in wearable technology enables personalized coaching, goal setting, and adaptive feedback to help users achieve their health and fitness objectives. The integration of AI has transformed wearable devices into comprehensive health and wellness companions, empowering individuals to make informed decisions about their lifestyle and activities.

AI in Entertainment and Media

AI has revolutionized the entertainment and media industry, influencing content creation, distribution, and user engagement. Recommendation systems, content curation, and interactive experiences are key areas where AI has made a significant impact.

Recommendation Systems

Streaming platforms, e-commerce websites, and social media networks leverage AI-powered recommendation systems to personalize content and product suggestions for users. These systems analyze user preferences, behavior, and historical interactions to deliver tailored recommendations, thereby enhancing user satisfaction and engagement.

AI algorithms continuously learn from user feedback and interactions to refine the accuracy and relevance of recommendations, creating a dynamic and personalized content discovery experience for consumers.

Content Creation and Curation

AI technologies, such as natural language processing and generative models, are employed in content creation and curation processes. Automated content generation, including news articles, product descriptions, and creative writing, is facilitated by AI algorithms that can mimic human language and style.

Additionally, AI-powered curation tools assist media organizations and content platforms in sorting, categorizing, and recommending content based on user preferences and trending topics. These tools optimize content delivery and consumption experiences, catering to diverse audience interests and consumption patterns.

Interactive Experiences

AI-driven interactive experiences, such as virtual reality (VR) and augmented reality (AR) applications, have redefined user engagement and immersion in entertainment and media. These technologies utilize AI for spatial recognition, object tracking, and real-time rendering, enabling captivating and interactive experiences for users.

Furthermore, AI-enhanced interactive storytelling and gaming experiences leverage machine learning and natural language processing to adapt narratives, character behaviors, and gameplay dynamics based on user input and preferences, creating personalized and engaging entertainment experiences.

AI in Transportation

The transportation sector has witnessed transformative advancements through the integration of AI, particularly in the domains of autonomous vehicles, traffic management systems, and navigation optimization.

Autonomous Vehicles

AI serves as the cornerstone of autonomous vehicle technology, enabling vehicles to perceive their surroundings, make real-time decisions, and navigate complex environments without human intervention. Machine learning algorithms and sensor fusion techniques empower autonomous vehicles to interpret and respond to dynamic road conditions, ensuring safe and efficient transportation.

The development of autonomous vehicles has the potential to revolutionize mobility, improve road safety, and enhance accessibility for individuals with mobility challenges, marking a significant milestone in the evolution of transportation technology.

Traffic Management Systems

AI-driven traffic management systems leverage data analytics and predictive modeling to optimize traffic flow, reduce congestion, and enhance overall transportation efficiency. These systems utilize real-time data from various sources, including traffic cameras, sensors, and connected vehicles, to dynamically adjust signal timings, reroute traffic, and mitigate bottlenecks.

By harnessing AI, transportation authorities can proactively manage traffic patterns, respond to incidents, and improve the overall commuting experience for road users, contributing to sustainable and resilient urban mobility.

Navigation and Route Optimization

Navigation and route optimization applications integrate AI algorithms to provide users with intelligent and adaptive routing solutions. These applications consider real-time traffic conditions, historical travel patterns, and user preferences to offer optimal routes that minimize travel time and fuel consumption.

AI-powered navigation systems also incorporate predictive analysis to anticipate traffic disruptions, road closures, and weather-related challenges, empowering users to make informed decisions and navigate efficiently, thereby enhancing the overall travel experience.

AI in Healthcare

AI's impact on healthcare is profound, with applications ranging from medical imaging and diagnosis to personalized medicine and health monitoring devices. These advancements have the potential to improve patient care, enhance diagnostic accuracy, and empower individuals to take proactive control of their health.

Medical Imaging and Diagnosis

AI algorithms are revolutionizing medical imaging interpretation by enabling automated analysis of radiological images, such as X-rays, MRIs, and CT scans. These algorithms can detect anomalies, assist in early disease detection, and provide quantitative insights to healthcare professionals, thereby improving diagnostic accuracy and expediting treatment decisions.

Furthermore, AI-powered diagnostic tools have the potential to address healthcare disparities by providing access to expert-level diagnostic capabilities in resource-constrained settings, ultimately improving patient outcomes and reducing the burden on healthcare systems.

Personalized Medicine

AI plays a pivotal role in advancing personalized medicine, leveraging patient data, genetic information, and clinical insights to tailor treatment plans and interventions based on individual characteristics and disease profiles. Machine learning models analyze diverse datasets to identify personalized treatment options, predict treatment responses, and optimize therapeutic strategies.

By embracing AI-driven personalized medicine, healthcare providers can deliver targeted and effective interventions, minimize adverse effects, and optimize patient outcomes, ushering in a new era of precision healthcare delivery.

Health Monitoring Devices

Wearable health monitoring devices equipped with AI capabilities enable continuous tracking of vital signs, activity levels, and physiological parameters, empowering individuals to monitor their health in real time. These devices utilize AI algorithms to detect patterns, anomalies, and trends, providing users with actionable insights and early warnings related to their well-being.

Moreover, AI-powered health monitoring devices can facilitate remote patient monitoring, chronic disease management, and proactive health interventions, fostering a paradigm shift towards preventive and personalized healthcare at the individual level.

Review Questions

1. Which of the following is an example of AI in personal devices?

    A. Smartphones and Virtual Assistants

    B. Recommendation Systems

    C. Autonomous Vehicles

2. What type of AI is used for content creation and curation in entertainment and media?

    A. Medical Imaging and Diagnosis

B. Content Creation and Curation

C. Health Monitoring Devices

3. Which area of AI in transportation involves optimizing navigation routes?

   A. Navigation and Route Optimization

   B. Autonomous Vehicles

   C. Traffic Management Systems

4. In healthcare, what does AI use for personalized treatment?

   A. Personalized Medicine

   B. Interactive Experiences

   C. Wearable Technology

5. What is an example of AI in healthcare for medical diagnosis?

   A. Smart Home Devices

   B. Medical Imaging and Diagnosis

   C. Recommendation System

CHAPTER 14

Ethical Considerations in AI

Understanding Ethical Issues in AI

Ethical considerations in artificial intelligence (AI) are of paramount importance as AI systems increasingly impact various aspects of our lives. The ethical issues in AI encompass a wide range of concerns, including bias and fairness, privacy and data protection, as well as transparency and accountability.

Bias and Fairness

Bias in AI refers to the systematic and unfair preferences or prejudices that can be present in AI algorithms, leading to discriminatory outcomes. This bias can stem from the data used to train AI systems, the algorithms' design, or the AI systems' decision-making processes. Fairness in AI involves ensuring that the outcomes and decisions made by AI systems are unbiased and equitable for all individuals and groups, regardless of their characteristics.

Addressing bias and fairness in AI requires careful examination of the data used for training, the design of algorithms, and the evaluation of AI system outputs. It also involves developing techniques to detect and mitigate biases in AI systems and establishing standards for fairness in AI applications.

Privacy and Data Protection

Privacy and data protection are critical ethical considerations in AI, particularly as AI systems often rely on large volumes of personal and sensitive data. The collection, storage, and processing of data by AI systems raise concerns about individuals' privacy rights and the potential misuse of their personal information.

Ensuring privacy and data protection in AI involves implementing robust data governance practices, including data anonymization, encryption, and secure data storage. It also requires adherence to regulations and standards related to data privacy, such as the General Data Protection Regulation (GDPR) in the European Union and the development of AI systems that prioritize data security and user privacy.

Transparency and Accountability

Transparency and accountability are essential for building trust in AI systems and ensuring that their decision-making processes are understandable and justifiable. Transparency involves making AI systems' operations and decision-making processes accessible and comprehensible to stakeholders, including users, regulators, and affected individuals. Accountability in AI pertains to the responsibility of AI developers, deployers, and users for the outcomes and impacts of AI systems.

To promote transparency and accountability in AI, efforts should be made to enhance AI algorithms' explainability and decision-making processes. This may involve developing interpretable AI models and establishing mechanisms for auditing and reviewing AI system decisions.

Impact on Employment and Society

The widespread adoption of AI technologies has significant implications for employment and society, raising concerns about job displacement, economic inequality, and broader social impacts.

Job Displacement

The automation of tasks and processes through AI technologies has the potential to lead to job displacement in various industries. As AI systems become capable of performing tasks traditionally carried out by humans, there is a risk of certain jobs becoming obsolete, impacting the livelihoods of workers in those roles.

Addressing the potential job displacement caused by AI requires proactive measures, such as reskilling and upskilling programs to prepare workers for new roles, as well as the creation of policies and initiatives to support displaced workers in transitioning to new employment opportunities.

Economic Inequality

The impact of AI on employment and the distribution of wealth can contribute to economic inequality within societies. The automation of certain jobs may lead to disparities in income and opportunities, potentially widening the gap between different socioeconomic groups.

To mitigate economic inequality resulting from AI adoption, it is essential to consider policies and interventions aimed at ensuring equitable access to education, training, and employment opportunities. Additionally, measures to promote inclusive economic growth and support marginalized communities in adapting to technological changes are crucial.

Social Impact

The broader social impact of AI encompasses its effects on social dynamics, community well-being, and society's overall fabric. AI technologies can influence social interactions, cultural norms, and the distribution of power and resources within communities.

Understanding and addressing AI's social impact requires interdisciplinary collaboration and engagement with diverse stakeholders, including community representatives, social scientists, and policymakers. It involves considering AI adoption's ethical and societal implications and ensuring that AI technologies contribute positively to social cohesion and well-being.

Ethical Decision-Making in AI

Ethical decision-making in AI involves developing and applying frameworks, guidelines, and practices that prioritize ethical considerations throughout the lifecycle of AI systems, from design and development to deployment and use.

Ethical Frameworks and Guidelines

Establishing ethical frameworks and guidelines for AI involves defining principles and standards that guide the responsible and ethical development and use of AI technologies. These frameworks may encompass principles such as fairness, transparency, accountability, and the protection of human rights in the context of AI applications.

Developing and adhering to ethical frameworks and guidelines requires collaboration among AI developers, ethicists, policymakers, and representatives from affected communities to ensure that AI technologies align with ethical norms and values.

Responsible AI Development

Responsible AI development involves integrating ethical considerations into the design and implementation of AI systems, prioritizing the well-being and rights of individuals and communities affected by AI technologies. It encompasses practices such as ethical design thinking, risk assessment, and the incorporation of ethical impact assessments into the development process.

Promoting responsible AI development requires a commitment to ethical best practices, ongoing evaluation of AI system impacts, and the cultivation of a culture of ethical awareness and responsibility within AI development teams.

Ethical Use of AI in Decision-Making

The ethical use of AI in decision-making involves ensuring that AI systems are deployed and utilized in ways that uphold ethical principles and respect the rights and dignity of individuals. This includes considerations of the potential impacts of AI decisions on individuals and communities, as well as the ethical implications of automated decision-making processes.

Integrating ethical considerations into the use of AI requires ongoing monitoring, evaluation, and refinement of AI applications to align with ethical norms and values. It also involves fostering ethical awareness and accountability among AI system users and stakeholders.

Regulation and Governance

Regulation and governance play a crucial role in shaping the ethical landscape of AI, providing the legal and institutional frameworks necessary to ensure that AI technologies are developed, deployed, and used in a manner that upholds ethical standards and societal values.

Government Policies and Legislation

Government policies and legislation related to AI aim to establish regulatory frameworks that address ethical considerations, data privacy, transparency, and accountability in AI development and deployment. These policies may include guidelines for the ethical use of AI, requirements for transparency in AI decision-making, and mechanisms for oversight and enforcement.

Developing and implementing effective government policies and legislation requires collaboration between policymakers, legal experts, technologists, and representatives from affected communities to ensure that regulatory frameworks align with ethical principles and societal needs.

Industry Standards and Best Practices

Industry standards and best practices for AI governance involve the development of guidelines, certifications, and industry-led initiatives that promote ethical and responsible AI development and use. These standards may encompass principles of fairness, transparency, and accountability, as well as mechanisms for ethical impact assessment and reporting.

Engaging with industry stakeholders, professional associations, and standards-setting bodies is essential for establishing and promoting industry standards and best practices that prioritize ethical considerations in AI technologies.

International Collaboration

International collaboration in AI governance involves coordination among countries, international organizations, and global stakeholders to address ethical considerations and regulatory challenges in the development and deployment of AI technologies. This collaboration may include the harmonization of ethical standards, the sharing of best practices, and the establishment of mechanisms for cross-border oversight and cooperation.

Promoting international collaboration in AI governance requires diplomatic engagement, multilateral dialogue, and the alignment of ethical priorities and regulatory approaches across diverse geopolitical and cultural contexts.

Review Questions

1. What are some ethical issues in AI?

    A. Job Displacement

    B. Economic Inequality

    C. Bias and Fairness

D. Social Impact

2. Which of the following is an impact of AI on employment and society?

   A. Responsible AI Development

   B. Transparency and Accountability

   C. Job Displacement

   D. Government Policies and Legislation

3. What is an example of ethical decision-making in AI?

   A. International Collaboration

   B. Industry Standards and Best Practices

   C. Economic Inequality

   D. Responsible AI Development

4. What does regulation and governance in AI involve?

   A. Social Impact

   B. Government Policies and Legislation

   C. Ethical Use of AI in Decision-Making

   D. Bias and Fairness

5. Which of the following is a key aspect of ethical decision-making in AI?

   A. Impact on Employment

   B. Responsible AI Development

CHAPTER 15

Future of AI

Advancements in AI Technology

Advancements in AI technology are continuously shaping the future of artificial intelligence. Machine learning innovations, natural language processing breakthroughs, and robotics and automation developments are at the forefront of driving AI into new frontiers.

Machine Learning Innovations

Machine learning, a subset of AI that enables systems to learn and improve from experience without explicit programming, is witnessing remarkable innovations. The future of machine learning holds the promise of more efficient algorithms, enhanced model interpretability, and the ability to handle complex and unstructured data with greater accuracy.

New techniques such as reinforcement learning, transfer learning, and federated learning are expanding the capabilities of machine learning systems. These innovations are paving the way for AI applications that can adapt and learn in real-time, leading to more personalized user experiences and improved decision-making processes.

Natural Language Processing Breakthroughs

Natural language processing (NLP) is undergoing significant breakthroughs, driven by advancements in deep learning models and large-scale language understanding. The future of NLP holds the potential for more nuanced language understanding, improved sentiment analysis, and the ability to comprehend and generate human-like text with higher accuracy.

With the development of transformer-based models and pre-trained language representations, NLP systems are becoming more adept at understanding context, tone, and nuances in human language. These breakthroughs are revolutionizing the way AI interacts with and processes natural language, leading to more sophisticated chatbots, language translation systems, and content-generation tools.

Robotics and Automation Developments

The field of robotics and automation is experiencing rapid advancements driven by AI technologies such as computer vision, reinforcement learning, and sensor integration. The future of robotics holds the promise of more autonomous and adaptive robotic systems capable of performing complex tasks in unstructured environments with precision and efficiency.

From collaborative robots (cobots) that can work alongside humans in manufacturing settings to autonomous drones and vehicles that can navigate and make decisions in dynamic environments, AI-powered robotics are reshaping industries and opening new possibilities for automation. These developments are not only enhancing productivity and safety but also expanding the role of robotics in areas such as healthcare, logistics, and infrastructure maintenance.

Integration of AI in Various Industries

The integration of AI in various industries is poised to transform the way businesses operate, deliver services, and innovate. Healthcare and medicine, finance and banking, and education and learning are among the sectors where AI is expected to have a profound impact in the future.

Healthcare and Medicine

In the healthcare and medical industry, AI is anticipated to revolutionize disease diagnosis, treatment planning, and patient care. From AI-powered medical imaging analysis and predictive analytics for early disease detection to personalized treatment recommendations and remote patient monitoring, the integration of AI is expected to improve healthcare outcomes and enhance the delivery of medical services.

Furthermore, AI-driven drug discovery and development, as well as the use of machine learning algorithms for precision medicine, hold the potential to accelerate the development of new therapies and improve the efficacy of treatments for various medical conditions.

Finance and Banking

The integration of AI technologies is significantly transforming the finance and banking sector. From algorithmic trading and fraud detection to personalized financial advice and risk management, AI is reshaping the way financial institutions operate, make decisions, and interact with customers.

The future of AI in finance promises more efficient and accurate predictive modeling, enhanced customer service through AI-powered chatbots and virtual assistants, and the development of innovative financial products and services driven by machine learning algorithms and data analytics.

Education and Learning

In the field of education and learning, AI integration is expected to revolutionize personalized learning experiences, teacher support and development, and administrative efficiency. AI-powered adaptive learning platforms, automated grading systems, and personalized lesson planning tools are poised to enhance the way students learn and educators teach.

Furthermore, the integration of AI in education holds the potential to streamline administrative tasks, improve resource allocation, and provide tailored support for students with diverse learning needs. AI technologies are expected to play a pivotal role in shaping the future of education and learning, making education more accessible, personalized, and effective.

Ethical and Societal Implications

As AI technologies continue to advance, it is crucial to consider the ethical and societal implications of these advancements. The interaction between humans and AI, ethical AI governance, and the social impact of AI advancements are key areas of concern that require careful consideration and proactive measures.

AI and Human interaction

The future of AI raises important questions about the nature of human-AI interaction, including issues related to trust, transparency, and the ethical use of AI in decision-making processes. As AI systems become more integrated into various aspects of society, understanding and shaping the dynamics of human-AI interaction will be essential for fostering trust and ensuring responsible AI deployment.

Furthermore, the development of AI systems that prioritize user well-being, respect privacy, and promote transparent communication will be critical in shaping the future of human-AI interaction and fostering positive societal outcomes.

Ethical AI Governance

Ethical AI governance encompasses the development of frameworks, guidelines, and regulations that ensure the responsible and ethical use of AI technologies. As AI continues to advance, it is imperative to establish ethical standards and governance mechanisms that address issues such as bias and fairness, privacy and data protection, and accountability in AI decision-making.

The future of AI governance will require collaboration between policymakers, industry stakeholders, and ethicists to develop and

implement ethical AI principles that safeguard societal values and
promote the responsible development and deployment of AI
technologies.

Social Impact of AI Advancements

The societal impact of AI advancements extends to areas such as
employment, education, healthcare, and public policy. As AI
technologies reshape industries and transform the way we live and
work, it is essential to consider the broader social implications of these
advancements, including issues related to job displacement, economic
inequality, and access to AI-driven services and opportunities.

Addressing the social impact of AI advancements will require
proactive measures to mitigate potential negative consequences and
ensure that AI technologies contribute to a more equitable, inclusive,
and sustainable future for society as a whole.

Challenges and Opportunities

While the future of AI presents numerous opportunities for innovation
and progress, it also brings forth a set of challenges that must be
addressed to realize the full potential of AI technologies. Addressing
bias and fairness, navigating the evolution of the job market, and
fostering innovation and creativity in AI are among the key challenges
and opportunities that lie ahead.

Addressing Bias and Fairness

One of the critical challenges in the future of AI is addressing bias and ensuring fairness in AI systems. As AI technologies are increasingly used to make decisions that impact individuals and communities, it is essential to mitigate biases in data, algorithms, and decision-making processes to ensure equitable outcomes and prevent discriminatory practices.

Opportunities for addressing bias and fairness in AI lie in the development of inclusive and diverse datasets, the implementation of bias detection and mitigation techniques, and the promotion of ethical AI principles that prioritize fairness, transparency, and accountability.

Job Market Evolution

The evolution of the job market in the context of AI advancements presents both challenges and opportunities. While AI technologies have the potential to automate routine tasks and create new job opportunities in emerging fields, they also raise concerns about job displacement, skills retraining, and the future of work in an AI-driven economy.

Navigating the job market evolution in the future of AI will require proactive measures to reskill and upskill the workforce, foster entrepreneurship and innovation, and create supportive policies and programs that enable individuals to adapt to the changing demands of the labor market.

Innovation and Creativity in AI

Fostering innovation and creativity in AI is essential for driving continued advancements and unlocking the full potential of AI technologies. The future of AI presents opportunities to explore new frontiers in AI research, develop novel applications that address societal challenges, and promote interdisciplinary collaboration that fuels innovation and creativity.

Challenges in fostering innovation and creativity in AI include the need for diverse perspectives and expertise, the ethical considerations of AI-driven innovation, and the responsible development and deployment of AI technologies that prioritize positive societal impact and ethical considerations.

Review Questions

1. Which of the following is a key area of advancement in AI technology discussed in the chapter?

    A. Robotics and Automation Developments

    B. Virtual Reality Applications

    C. 3D Printing Innovations

2. In which of the following industries is AI integration discussed in the chapter?

    A. Tourism and Hospitality

    B. Finance and Banking

    C. Agriculture and Farming

3. What is one of the ethical implications of AI discussed in the chapter?

    A. Marine Biology and AI

B. AI and Human-AI Interaction

C. Space Exploration and AI

4. What is a challenge related to AI discussed in the chapter?

    A. Weather Forecasting Accuracy

    B. Addressing Bias and Fairness

    C. Traffic Management Efficiency

5. Which of the following is considered an opportunity in AI, according to the chapter?

    A. Decrease in Environmental Awareness

    B. Job Market Evolution

    C. Decline in Technological Innovation

CHAPTER 16

AI and Automation

Understanding Automation and AI

Automation refers to the use of technology and machinery to perform tasks with minimal human intervention. It aims to streamline processes, increase efficiency, and reduce human error. The history of automation can be traced back to the Industrial Revolution when machines were first introduced to perform repetitive tasks in manufacturing.

With the advancement of technology, automation has evolved to encompass a wide range of industries and processes, from assembly lines in factories to data entry in offices. The integration of artificial intelligence (AI) in automation has further revolutionized the way tasks are performed, allowing for more complex decision-making and adaptive processes.

AI's role in automation involves using algorithms and machine learning models to enable systems to learn from data, make predictions, and optimize processes. This combination of AI and automation has led to the development of intelligent systems capable of autonomous decision-making and adaptive behavior.

Applications of AI in Automation

AI has found numerous applications in the field of automation, transforming traditional processes and revolutionizing industries. Some of the key applications of AI in automation include:

Manufacturing and Production

In manufacturing, AI-powered automation systems are used to optimize production processes, improve quality control, and enhance overall efficiency. AI algorithms analyze production data in real-time to identify patterns, predict equipment failures, and optimize production schedules. This leads to reduced downtime, improved product quality, and increased output.

Supply Chain Management

AI plays a crucial role in automating supply chain processes, including demand forecasting, inventory management, and logistics optimization. By analyzing large volumes of data, AI systems can predict demand patterns, optimize inventory levels, and streamline the movement of goods, leading to cost savings and improved customer satisfaction.

Quality Control and Inspection

AI-powered automation systems are used for quality control and inspection in various industries, including manufacturing, agriculture, and healthcare. Machine learning algorithms analyze visual data to detect defects, anomalies, or irregularities in products, ensuring that only high-quality items reach the market. This not only improves product quality but also reduces waste and rework.

Impact on the Workforce

The integration of AI in automation has significant implications for the workforce, leading to changes in job roles, skills requirements, and labor market dynamics.

Job Transformation

AI-powered automation has led to the transformation of traditional job roles, with some tasks being automated while new roles requiring AI-related skills emerge. For example, repetitive manual tasks in manufacturing may be automated, leading to the creation of roles focused on managing and maintaining automated systems.

Skills and Training Needs

The adoption of AI in automation has increased the demand for skills related to data analysis, machine learning, and programming. As automation systems become more sophisticated, there is a growing need for workers who can understand, operate, and optimize these systems. This has led to an increased emphasis on training and upskilling the workforce.

Labor Market Dynamics

The introduction of AI-powered automation has reshaped the labor market, with certain industries experiencing shifts in demand for specific skills. While some traditional roles may decline, new opportunities in AI-related fields, such as data science and AI engineering, have emerged. This has led to a reevaluation of workforce planning and skill development strategies.

Societal and Economic Implications

The widespread adoption of AI-powered automation has far-reaching implications for society and the economy, influencing factors such as economic efficiency, income inequality, and work-life balance.

Economic Efficiency and Productivity

AI-powered automation has the potential to significantly improve economic efficiency and productivity by streamlining processes, reducing waste, and optimizing resource allocation. This can lead to cost savings for businesses, increased output, and overall economic growth.

Income Inequality

While AI-powered automation can create new opportunities and higher-skilled jobs, it also has the potential to exacerbate income inequality. Workers in roles that are easily automated may face job displacement, while those with AI-related skills may benefit from higher wages and increased demand for their expertise.

Work-Life Balance

The introduction of AI-powered automation has the potential to redefine work-life balance by automating repetitive and mundane tasks, allowing workers to focus on more creative and strategic aspects of their roles. However, it also raises questions about the impact of automation on job satisfaction and the nature of work.

Review Questions

1. What is the role of AI in automation?

    A. Eliminating the need for automation

    B. Enhancing human capabilities

    C. Replacing human workers

2. Which of the following is an application of AI in automation?

    A. Customer service management

    B. Quality control and inspection

C. Social media marketing

3. What is one impact of AI and automation on the workforce?

   A. Job transformation

   B. Decreased economic efficiency

   C. Reduced need for skills and training

4. What is one societal implication of AI and automation?

   A. Decreased economic productivity

   B. Income inequality

   C. Increased work-life balance

5. In the history of automation, what has been the role of AI?

   A. AI has always been the primary driver of automation

   B. AI has played a minimal role in automation

   C. AI has increasingly become integrated into automation processes

CHAPTER 17

AI and Robotics

Integration of AI and Robotics

AI and robotics have become increasingly integrated, leading to advancements in various fields. Collaborative robotics, autonomous systems, and human-robot interaction are key areas where AI plays a crucial role.

Collaborative Robotics

Collaborative robotics, also known as cobots, are designed to work alongside humans in a shared workspace. These robots are equipped with advanced sensors and AI algorithms that enable them to detect and respond to human presence, ensuring safe and efficient collaboration. The integration of AI allows cobots to adapt to dynamic environments and perform tasks that require close interaction with human workers.

One of the key benefits of collaborative robotics is the ability to enhance productivity and flexibility in manufacturing processes. These robots can assist human workers in tasks that are repetitive, strenuous, or pose safety risks. With AI-driven capabilities, cobots can learn from human behavior and adjust their actions to optimize workflow and minimize errors.

Autonomous Systems

Autonomous robotic systems leverage AI to operate independently, making decisions based on real-time data and environmental inputs. These systems are used in various domains, including transportation, logistics, and exploration. AI algorithms enable autonomous robots to navigate complex environments, adapt to changing conditions, and execute tasks with minimal human intervention.

In the field of autonomous vehicles, AI plays a critical role in perception, decision-making, and control. Self-driving cars, drones, and unmanned aerial vehicles (UAVs) rely on AI to interpret sensor data, identify obstacles, and plan optimal routes. The integration of AI in autonomous systems has the potential to revolutionize industries by improving efficiency, safety, and resource utilization.

Human-Robot Interaction

Human-robot interaction (HRI) focuses on the design and implementation of robotic systems that can effectively communicate and collaborate with humans. AI technologies such as natural language processing, gesture recognition, and affective computing enable robots to understand and respond to human input in a meaningful way. This interaction is essential in scenarios where robots assist individuals in daily tasks, healthcare, and social settings.

Advancements in AI have led to the development of socially intelligent robots capable of recognizing human emotions, adapting their behavior, and providing empathetic support. These robots are designed to engage in natural and intuitive interactions, fostering trust and acceptance among users. The integration of AI in HRI is shaping the future of assistive and companion robotics, offering new possibilities for human-robot collaboration.

Applications of AI in Robotics

AI's applications in robotics span diverse industries, driving innovation and efficiency in manufacturing, healthcare, and agriculture. From precision assembly to medical assistance, AI-powered robots are transforming traditional processes and expanding robotic systems' capabilities.

Manufacturing and Assembly

AI-enabled robots are revolutionizing production lines in manufacturing and assembly by automating complex tasks, ensuring quality control, and enhancing operational agility. These robots are equipped with advanced vision systems, adaptive grasping mechanisms, and predictive maintenance capabilities, enabling them to handle intricate assembly processes with precision and speed.

The integration of AI in manufacturing robotics also facilitates adaptive manufacturing, where robots can reconfigure their actions based on real-time feedback and production requirements. This flexibility allows for rapid customization, efficient resource utilization, and seamless integration of robotic systems into diverse manufacturing environments.

Healthcare and Medical Robotics

AI-driven robotics has significant implications for healthcare, offering solutions for surgical assistance, rehabilitation, and patient care. Surgical robots equipped with AI algorithms can enhance the precision and safety of medical procedures, leading to improved outcomes and reduced recovery times. These robots can analyze medical imaging data, assist in complex surgeries, and provide real-time feedback to medical professionals.

Medical robotics also extends to applications such as telemedicine, where AI-powered robots enable remote diagnosis, monitoring, and personalized care delivery. The integration of AI in healthcare robotics is paving the way for advanced medical interventions, personalized treatment plans, and accessible healthcare services for diverse populations.

Agricultural Robotics

AI-powered agricultural robotics are transforming traditional farming practices by enabling precision agriculture, autonomous harvesting, and crop monitoring. AI-driven robots equipped with sensors and machine learning algorithms can assess crop health, optimize irrigation, and perform targeted interventions, leading to improved yield and resource efficiency.

The integration of AI in agricultural robotics also addresses labor shortages and the need for sustainable farming practices. These robots can autonomously navigate fields, identify and manage pests, and contribute to environmentally conscious farming methods. The advancements in agricultural robotics are reshaping the future of food production and contributing to global food security.

Challenges and Advancements

While the integration of AI in robotics brings about numerous benefits, it also presents challenges and opportunities for further advancements. Safety and ethical considerations, AI-driven robotic learning, and adaptability and flexibility are key areas that require attention and innovation.

Safety and Ethical Considerations

Ensuring the safety of AI-driven robotic systems is paramount, especially in collaborative and human-centric environments. Ethical considerations related to robot behavior, decision-making, and potential impact on human well-being need to be carefully addressed. Robotic safety standards, transparent AI algorithms, and ethical guidelines for robotic interactions are essential for building trust and ensuring responsible deployment of AI-powered robots.

Furthermore, ethical considerations extend to the use of AI in robotics for decision-making in critical scenarios, such as medical interventions and autonomous vehicles. The ethical implications of AI-driven robotic systems require interdisciplinary collaboration and continuous evaluation to mitigate risks and uphold ethical principles.

AI-Driven Robotic Learning

The field of AI-driven robotic learning focuses on enabling robots to acquire new skills, adapt to novel environments, and learn from human demonstrations. Reinforcement learning, imitation learning, and transfer learning are key paradigms that empower robots to continuously improve their capabilities and performance. The integration of AI in robotic learning is essential for developing versatile and adaptive robotic systems that can operate in dynamic and unstructured settings.

Challenges in AI-driven robotic learning include addressing sample efficiency, generalization to diverse tasks, and safe exploration in real-world environments. Advancements in AI algorithms and robotic learning frameworks are driving progress in creating robots that can autonomously acquire and refine their skills, leading to more capable and versatile robotic systems.

Adaptability and Flexibility

AI-powered robots need to exhibit adaptability and flexibility to effectively operate in dynamic and unstructured environments. The ability to handle unforeseen events, adjust to changing conditions, and collaborate with human partners requires advanced AI capabilities. Robotic systems that can learn from experience, interpret ambiguous inputs, and dynamically reconfigure their actions are essential for addressing real-world challenges.

Advancements in AI for robotic adaptability and flexibility encompass areas such as multi-modal sensor fusion, context-aware decision-making, and human-aware planning. These advancements enable robots to seamlessly integrate into diverse settings, interact with human collaborators, and perform tasks with agility and responsiveness.

Review Questions

1. What are the main areas of integration of AI and Robotics?

    A. Collaborative Robotics, Autonomous Systems, and Human-Robot Interaction

B. Manufacturing and Assembly, Healthcare and Medical Robotics, and Agricultural Robotics

C. Safety and Ethical Considerations, AI-Driven Robotic Learning, and Adaptability and Flexibility

2. Which of the following are applications of AI in Robotics?

A. Safety and Ethical Considerations, AI-Driven Robotic Learning, and Adaptability and Flexibility

B. Manufacturing and Assembly, Healthcare and Medical Robotics, and Agricultural Robotics

C. Collaborative Robotics, Autonomous Systems, and Human-Robot Interaction

3. What are the main challenges and advancements in AI and Robotics?

A. Manufacturing and Assembly, Healthcare and Medical Robotics, and Agricultural Robotics

B. Collaborative Robotics, Autonomous Systems, and Human-Robot Interaction

C. Safety and Ethical Considerations, AI-Driven Robotic Learning, and Adaptability and Flexibility

4. Which of the following is not an area of integration of AI and Robotics?

A. Collaborative Robotics

B. Manufacturing and Assembly

C. Safety and Ethical Considerations

5. What type of robotics involves the use of AI for learning and decision-making?

A. Collaborative Robotics

B. Autonomous Systems

C. AI-Driven Robotic Learning

CHAPTER 18

AI and Healthcare

AI Applications in Healthcare

Artificial Intelligence (AI) has revolutionized the healthcare industry by offering innovative solutions to various challenges. The applications of AI in healthcare are diverse and impactful, ranging from medical imaging and diagnostics to drug discovery and personalized medicine.

Medical Imaging and Diagnostics

One of the most significant contributions of AI in healthcare is its role in medical imaging and diagnostics. AI-powered algorithms have demonstrated remarkable accuracy in interpreting medical images such as X-rays, MRIs, and CT scans. These algorithms can detect anomalies, identify patterns, and assist healthcare professionals in making more precise diagnoses.

Furthermore, AI has the potential to expedite the diagnostic process by analyzing large volumes of medical images in a fraction of the time it would take a human expert. This acceleration can be critical in emergency situations and can lead to more timely interventions and treatments.

Moreover, AI has shown promise in predicting disease progression and treatment outcomes based on imaging data. By analyzing subtle changes in medical images over time, AI algorithms can provide valuable insights for personalized treatment plans and monitoring of patient response to therapy.

Drug Discovery and Development

AI has significantly impacted the process of drug discovery and development, offering new avenues for innovation and efficiency. By leveraging machine learning and data analytics, AI can analyze vast datasets to identify potential drug candidates, predict their efficacy, and optimize their molecular structures.

Furthermore, AI algorithms can expedite the screening of compounds and their interactions with biological targets, leading to the identification of novel drug candidates with higher precision and speed. This acceleration in the drug discovery process has the potential to bring life-saving medications to patients more rapidly.

Additionally, AI plays a crucial role in repurposing existing drugs for new therapeutic applications. By analyzing diverse datasets and biological pathways, AI can identify opportunities for utilizing approved drugs in the treatment of different diseases, thereby reducing the time and resources required for drug development.

Personalized Medicine

Personalized medicine, also known as precision medicine, aims to tailor medical treatment and interventions to individual characteristics, including genetic makeup, lifestyle, and environmental factors. AI has emerged as a powerful tool in advancing personalized medicine by analyzing complex datasets and identifying personalized treatment strategies.

Through the integration of AI and genomics, healthcare providers can gain insights into an individual's genetic predispositions to certain diseases and their potential responses to specific medications. This information can guide the selection of personalized treatment regimens, minimizing adverse reactions and optimizing therapeutic outcomes.

Moreover, AI-driven predictive modeling can assess a patient's risk of developing certain conditions and guide proactive interventions to prevent or mitigate the progression of diseases. By considering a patient's unique genetic and environmental factors, AI contributes to the realization of personalized healthcare that is tailored to each individual's needs.

Patient Care and Management

AI technologies have transformed patient care and management by enabling remote monitoring and telemedicine, facilitating health records and data analysis, and supporting treatment planning and decision-making.

Remote Monitoring and Telemedicine

Remote monitoring and telemedicine have become increasingly prevalent with the integration of AI technologies. AI-powered remote monitoring systems can track patients' vital signs, medication adherence, and disease progression from the comfort of their homes, providing real-time data to healthcare providers for proactive interventions.

Telemedicine platforms, supported by AI algorithms, enable virtual consultations, remote diagnosis, and treatment recommendations, expanding access to healthcare services for individuals in remote or underserved areas. These platforms also offer opportunities for continuous monitoring and follow-up care, enhancing patient engagement and adherence to treatment plans.

Furthermore, AI-driven telemedicine solutions can analyze patient data to identify trends, predict exacerbations of chronic conditions, and alert healthcare providers to potential health risks, leading to timely interventions and improved patient outcomes.

Health Records and Data Analysis

AI has revolutionized health records and data analysis by streamlining the management of electronic health records (EHRs), extracting valuable insights from clinical data, and supporting evidence-based decision-making. AI algorithms can analyze large volumes of patient data to identify patterns, correlations, and predictive indicators for various health conditions.

Moreover, AI-powered data analysis can assist in identifying potential adverse drug reactions, predicting disease outbreaks, and optimizing resource allocation within healthcare facilities. By leveraging AI, healthcare organizations can harness the power of big data to drive operational efficiencies and improve patient care delivery.

Additionally, AI supports the integration of disparate data sources, including genomic data, imaging studies, and real-time patient monitoring, to provide a comprehensive view of an individual's health status and facilitate personalized treatment strategies.

Treatment Planning and Decision Support

AI technologies offer valuable support in treatment planning and decision-making by synthesizing complex clinical data, recommending evidence-based interventions, and assisting healthcare providers in formulating personalized treatment plans.

AI-driven decision support systems can analyze patient data, clinical guidelines, and medical literature to provide healthcare professionals with actionable insights and treatment recommendations. These systems can aid in identifying optimal medication regimens, predicting treatment responses, and minimizing the risk of medical errors.

Furthermore, AI supports the interpretation of diagnostic tests, assists in surgical planning, and contributes to the optimization of treatment pathways, ultimately enhancing the quality and safety of patient care.

Ethical and Regulatory Considerations

As AI continues to transform healthcare, it is essential to address ethical and regulatory considerations to ensure the responsible and ethical use of AI technologies in the delivery of healthcare services.

Data Privacy and Security

Protecting patient data privacy and ensuring the security of healthcare information are paramount in the era of AI-driven healthcare. Healthcare organizations must implement robust data encryption, access controls, and secure data storage practices to safeguard patient confidentiality and prevent unauthorized access to sensitive health information.

Furthermore, the ethical use of patient data for AI applications requires transparent consent processes, clear data governance frameworks, and adherence to regulatory standards such as the Health Insurance Portability and Accountability Act (HIPAA) in the United States and the General Data Protection Regulation (GDPR) in the European Union.

Clinical Decision Support Systems

The development and deployment of AI-powered clinical decision support systems necessitate careful validation, rigorous testing, and ongoing monitoring to ensure their accuracy, reliability, and alignment with clinical best practices. Ethical considerations in the design of these systems include transparency in decision-making processes, mitigation of algorithmic biases, and the establishment of clear accountability for clinical outcomes.

Healthcare providers must critically evaluate the recommendations generated by AI systems, maintain clinical autonomy in decision-making, and consider AI-driven insights as complementary tools that augment their expertise rather than replace their judgment.

Regulatory Approval and Compliance

Regulatory bodies play a crucial role in overseeing the ethical and safe deployment of AI technologies in healthcare. The approval and regulation of AI-driven medical devices, diagnostic algorithms, and treatment decision support systems require robust evaluation processes to ensure their safety, effectiveness, and adherence to ethical standards.

Healthcare organizations and technology developers must collaborate with regulatory agencies to navigate the complex landscape of AI regulation, adhere to quality standards, and demonstrate the clinical validity and utility of AI applications in healthcare before their widespread adoption.

Review Questions

1. Which of the following is an AI application in healthcare related to medical imaging and diagnostics?

    A. Drug Discovery

    B. Medical Imaging and Diagnostics

C. Remote Monitoring

D. Personalized Medicine

2. What does AI in healthcare use for patient care and management related to health records and data analysis?

    A. Treatment Planning

    B. Health Records

    C. Remote Monitoring

    D. Telemedicine

3. Which ethical and regulatory consideration in AI healthcare involves data privacy and security?

    A. Remote Monitoring

    B. Clinical Decision Support Systems

    C. Regulatory Approval

    D. Data Privacy and Security

4. In AI healthcare, what does AI use for patient care and management related to remote monitoring and telemedicine?

    A. Treatment Planning

    B. Telemedicine

    C. Health Records

    D. Data Analysis

5. Which AI application in healthcare involves drug discovery and development?

A. Personalized Medicine

B. Drug Discovery and Development

C. Medical Imaging and Diagnostics

D. Clinical Decision Support Systems

CHAPTER 19

AI and the Environment

Environmental Monitoring and Analysis

Environmental monitoring and analysis play a crucial role in understanding and addressing the impact of human activities on the environment. Artificial intelligence (AI) has emerged as a powerful tool in this domain, enabling advanced modeling, prediction, and assessment of environmental factors. By leveraging AI technologies, researchers and environmentalists can gain valuable insights into climate change, natural disasters, and ecosystem health.

Climate Change Modeling

Climate change modeling involves the use of AI algorithms to analyze historical climate data, simulate future scenarios, and predict the potential impact of climate change on various regions. AI-powered climate models can incorporate complex interactions between atmospheric, oceanic, and terrestrial processes, providing more accurate projections of temperature changes, precipitation patterns, and extreme weather events. These models are instrumental in informing policymakers and stakeholders about the urgency of mitigating climate change and adapting to its consequences.

Furthermore, AI enables the integration of diverse datasets, such as satellite imagery, weather observations, and climate simulations, to enhance the precision and reliability of climate models. Machine learning algorithms can identify patterns and trends within these datasets, leading to improved understanding of climate dynamics and the identification of early warning signs for potential environmental disruptions.

Natural Disaster Prediction

Natural disaster prediction harnesses AI capabilities to forecast events such as hurricanes, floods, wildfires, and earthquakes with greater accuracy and lead time. By analyzing historical disaster data, environmental conditions, and geographical features, AI algorithms can identify patterns and indicators that precede catastrophic events. This proactive approach allows for the implementation of early warning systems and evacuation plans, potentially saving lives and reducing the impact of natural disasters on communities and ecosystems.

AI-based prediction models continuously learn from new data, enabling them to adapt to evolving environmental conditions and improve their forecasting accuracy over time. Additionally, the integration of real-time sensor data and satellite observations further enhances the precision of natural disaster prediction, empowering authorities to make informed decisions in emergency response and disaster preparedness.

Ecosystem Health Assessment

Ecosystem health assessment involves the monitoring and evaluation of ecological systems to understand their resilience, biodiversity, and overall well-being. AI-driven analysis of environmental data, including species distribution, habitat changes, and ecosystem dynamics, enables scientists to assess the impact of human activities, climate change, and other stressors on natural habitats.

Machine learning algorithms can process vast amounts of ecological data to identify trends, anomalies, and potential ecological disturbances, aiding in the early detection of environmental degradation and the formulation of conservation strategies. Furthermore, AI facilitates the integration of remote sensing data and ecological models, allowing for comprehensive assessments of ecosystem health at local, regional, and global scales.

Resource Management and Conservation

Resource management and conservation are essential components of environmental stewardship, aiming to optimize the use of natural resources while minimizing negative impacts on the environment. AI technologies offer innovative solutions for sustainable resource management, including energy optimization, water quality monitoring, and wildlife protection and preservation.

Energy Optimization

Energy optimization involves the application of AI algorithms to enhance the efficiency of energy production, distribution, and consumption. AI-driven energy management systems can analyze energy usage patterns, predict demand fluctuations, and optimize the operation of power grids and renewable energy sources. By leveraging real-time data and predictive analytics, AI contributes to reducing energy waste, lowering carbon emissions, and promoting the transition to sustainable energy solutions.

Furthermore, AI plays a pivotal role in the development of smart grid technologies, enabling dynamic energy pricing, demand response mechanisms, and grid stability enhancements. These advancements support the integration of renewable energy resources and the establishment of resilient energy infrastructures that can adapt to changing environmental conditions and energy demands.

Water Quality Monitoring

Water quality monitoring utilizes AI-based sensors and analytical tools to assess the chemical, physical, and biological characteristics of water bodies. AI algorithms can detect pollutants, monitor changes in water quality parameters, and identify potential sources of contamination, contributing to the protection of aquatic ecosystems and public health.

By leveraging machine learning models, water quality monitoring systems can recognize abnormal patterns in water quality data, enabling early detection of environmental hazards and the implementation of targeted remediation measures. Additionally, AI facilitates the integration of remote sensing technologies and unmanned aquatic vehicles for comprehensive and real-time monitoring of water resources.

Wildlife Protection and Preservation

Wildlife protection and preservation efforts benefit from AI applications that support conservation initiatives, combat wildlife trafficking, and monitor endangered species. AI-powered tools, such as camera traps, acoustic sensors, and satellite imagery analysis, enable the monitoring of wildlife populations, habitat encroachment, and illegal activities that threaten biodiversity.

Machine learning algorithms can analyze vast amounts of wildlife data to identify behavioral patterns, migration routes, and ecological interactions, providing valuable insights for conservation planning and management. Furthermore, AI facilitates the development of predictive models for wildlife population dynamics, aiding in the formulation of evidence-based conservation strategies and the protection of vulnerable species.

Sustainable Development and Planning

Sustainable development and planning encompass the integration of environmental considerations into urban and regional development, infrastructure design, and natural resource utilization. AI technologies offer innovative solutions for promoting sustainable practices, including urban planning and infrastructure development, renewable energy integration, and waste management and recycling.

Urban Planning and Infrastructure

Urban planning and infrastructure development benefit from AI-driven simulations, data analysis, and predictive modeling to optimize land use, transportation systems, and urban resilience. AI algorithms can analyze demographic trends, traffic patterns, and environmental factors to inform the design of sustainable cities, efficient transportation networks, and resilient infrastructure that can withstand environmental challenges.

Furthermore, AI supports the development of smart city technologies, including energy-efficient buildings, intelligent transportation systems, and real-time monitoring of urban environmental parameters. These advancements contribute to the creation of livable, environmentally conscious urban environments that prioritize sustainability and quality of life.

Renewable Energy Integration

Renewable energy integration leverages AI technologies to optimize the deployment and operation of renewable energy systems, such as solar, wind, and hydroelectric power. AI algorithms can forecast renewable energy generation, manage energy storage systems, and optimize the integration of renewable resources into existing power grids, contributing to the reduction of greenhouse gas emissions and the promotion of clean energy solutions.

Moreover, AI facilitates the development of virtual power plants, demand-side management strategies, and grid-balancing mechanisms that enable the reliable and cost-effective integration of renewable energy sources. These advancements support the transition to a sustainable energy landscape and the reduction of reliance on fossil fuels.

Waste Management and Recycling

Waste management and recycling efforts benefit from AI applications that optimize waste collection, recycling processes, and resource recovery. AI-powered systems can analyze waste generation patterns, identify opportunities for recycling and reuse, and optimize the operation of waste management facilities to minimize environmental impact.

Machine learning algorithms enable the identification of recyclable materials, sorting of waste streams, and prediction of waste generation trends, leading to more efficient and sustainable waste management practices. Additionally, AI supports the development of circular economy models that prioritize resource conservation, waste reduction, and the promotion of sustainable consumption and production patterns.

Review Questions

1. Which of the following is an example of environmental monitoring and analysis in AI?

    A. Energy Optimization

    B. Climate Change Modeling

C. Renewable Energy Integration

2. What is an example of resource management and conservation in AI?

    A. Waste Management and Recycling

    B. Water Quality Monitoring

    C. Urban Planning and Infrastructure

3. Which of the following is related to sustainable development and planning in AI?

    A. Natural Disaster Prediction

    B. Renewable Energy Integration

    C. Ecosystem Health Assessment

4. What is an example of AI's role in sustainable development and planning?

    A. Wildlife Protection and Preservation

    B. Urban Planning and Infrastructure

    C. Climate Change Modeling

5. Which of the following is an example of AI's impact on wildlife protection and preservation?

    A. Energy Optimization

    B. Water Quality Monitoring

    C. Wildlife Protection and Preservation

CHAPTER 20

AI and Society

Impact on Employment and Workforce

As artificial intelligence and automation technologies continue to advance, there is a growing concern about the impact on employment and the workforce. The integration of AI in various industries has led to discussions about job displacement, the emergence of new job opportunities, and the transformation of workplaces.

Automation and Job Displacement

The automation of tasks and processes previously performed by humans has raised concerns about job displacement. Routine and repetitive tasks in manufacturing, customer service, and administrative roles are increasingly being automated, leading to potential job losses for individuals in these sectors. While automation can improve efficiency and productivity, it also poses challenges for workers whose roles are at risk of being replaced by AI-powered systems.

Furthermore, the impact of automation extends beyond manual labor to include white-collar professions such as data analysis, legal research, and financial services. As AI technologies become more adept at handling complex tasks, there is a possibility of displacement in knowledge-based professions as well.

New Job Opportunities

Despite concerns about job displacement, the integration of AI also presents new job opportunities in emerging fields related to AI development, data science, machine learning, and robotics. The demand for professionals with expertise in AI technologies, including AI ethicists, AI trainers, and AI system integrators, is on the rise. Additionally, the need for individuals who can interpret and analyze data generated by AI systems has created new roles in data science and analytics.

Moreover, the evolution of AI has led to the creation of roles focused on human-AI collaboration, where individuals work alongside AI systems to enhance productivity and decision-making. These collaborative roles require a blend of technical skills and domain expertise, offering new avenues for employment in the AI era.

Workplace Transformation

The integration of AI technologies is reshaping the traditional workplace environment, leading to transformations in organizational structures, job roles, and skill requirements. Organizations are reevaluating their workforce composition and skill sets to adapt to the changing landscape influenced by AI and automation.

Furthermore, the introduction of AI-powered tools and systems is altering the nature of work itself, with an emphasis on tasks that complement AI capabilities, such as problem-solving, creativity, and emotional intelligence. This shift in focus is driving the need for upskilling and reskilling initiatives to prepare the workforce for the evolving demands of AI-integrated workplaces.

Social and Cultural Implications

Beyond the economic impact, the widespread adoption of AI technologies has significant social and cultural implications. Ethical decision-making in AI, cultural diversity and bias, and the potential for human-AI collaboration are key areas of consideration in the societal impact of AI.

Ethical Decision-Making in AI

The ethical considerations surrounding AI encompass a wide range of issues, including fairness, transparency, accountability, and the impact of AI on human autonomy and decision-making. As AI systems become increasingly integrated into various aspects of society, ethical frameworks and guidelines are essential for ensuring that AI technologies are developed and deployed in a responsible and ethical manner.

Furthermore, the ethical implications of AI extend to decision-making processes within AI systems, particularly in contexts where AI algorithms influence critical outcomes, such as healthcare, criminal justice, and financial services. Addressing ethical concerns in AI requires a multidisciplinary approach that involves input from ethicists, technologists, policymakers, and the broader community.

Cultural Diversity and Bias

The development and deployment of AI systems raise important considerations related to cultural diversity and bias. AI algorithms and models trained on biased or limited datasets can perpetuate and amplify existing societal biases, leading to discriminatory outcomes in areas such as hiring, lending, and law enforcement.

Recognizing and mitigating bias in AI requires a concerted effort to diversify datasets, incorporate ethical considerations into algorithm design, and promote inclusive practices in AI development. Additionally, fostering cultural diversity in AI research and development teams is crucial for addressing bias and ensuring that AI technologies serve diverse global populations equitably.

Human-AI Collaboration

The potential for collaboration between humans and AI systems presents opportunities for enhancing productivity, creativity, and decision-making. Human-AI collaboration involves leveraging the strengths of both humans and AI technologies to achieve synergistic outcomes that capitalize on human intuition, empathy, and contextual understanding, combined with AI's computational power and data processing capabilities.

Effective human-AI collaboration requires thoughtful design of AI interfaces, clear communication of AI system capabilities and limitations, and the establishment of trust between humans and AI systems. As AI technologies continue to evolve, the dynamics of human-AI collaboration will shape the future of work, creativity, and problem-solving in various domains.

Education and Training

The integration of AI in society necessitates a reevaluation of education and training paradigms to equip individuals with the skills and knowledge required to thrive in an AI-driven world. AI literacy, curriculum integration, skill development, and reskilling initiatives are essential components of preparing the workforce for the challenges and opportunities presented by AI.

AI Literacy and Curriculum Integration

AI literacy, encompassing an understanding of AI concepts, applications, and ethical considerations, is becoming increasingly important for individuals across diverse fields and disciplines. Integrating AI education into school curricula, vocational training programs, and higher education courses is essential for fostering AI literacy and preparing future generations for the AI-powered workforce.

Furthermore, AI literacy initiatives should emphasize critical thinking, ethical reasoning, and the societal implications of AI, enabling individuals to engage thoughtfully with AI technologies and contribute to informed decision-making in their personal and professional lives.

Skill Development and Reskilling

The rapid evolution of AI technologies necessitates ongoing skill development and reskilling efforts to ensure that the workforce remains adaptable and competitive. Individuals in industries affected by automation and AI integration may need to acquire new technical skills, such as data analysis, programming, and AI system management, to transition into emerging roles and fields.

Reskilling initiatives, supported by educational institutions, employers, and government programs, play a crucial role in facilitating the transition of workers into AI-related roles and addressing skill gaps in the workforce. Lifelong learning and continuous skill development are essential for navigating the dynamic landscape shaped by AI and automation.

AI in Educational Technology

The use of AI in educational technology, including adaptive learning platforms, personalized tutoring systems, and AI-driven educational content, has the potential to enhance the effectiveness and accessibility of education. AI-powered tools can provide personalized learning experiences, identify individual learning needs, and offer real-time feedback to students and educators.

Furthermore, AI technologies can support educators in developing tailored instructional materials, assessing student progress, and optimizing teaching strategies based on data-driven insights. Integrating AI in educational technology requires thoughtful consideration of ethical implications, data privacy, and the equitable distribution of AI-enhanced educational resources.

Public Policy and Governance

The ethical, legal, and regulatory dimensions of AI necessitate robust public policy and governance frameworks to ensure the responsible development, deployment, and use of AI technologies. Regulation and accountability, privacy and data protection, and the establishment of AI ethics and standards are critical aspects of shaping the societal impact of AI.

Regulation and Accountability

Effective regulation of AI technologies involves establishing clear guidelines, standards, and oversight mechanisms to address ethical, safety, and fairness considerations. Regulatory frameworks should encompass AI development, deployment, and use across diverse sectors, including healthcare, finance, transportation, and public services.

Furthermore, fostering accountability in AI requires transparency in AI system operations, mechanisms for addressing algorithmic bias and discrimination, and avenues for recourse in the event of AI-related harm or ethical violations. Collaboration between policymakers, industry stakeholders, and the public is essential for developing agile and adaptive regulatory approaches that keep pace with AI advancements.

Privacy and Data Protection

The proliferation of AI technologies raises significant privacy and data protection concerns related to the collection, storage, and utilization of personal and sensitive data. Safeguarding individual privacy and ensuring responsible data practices in AI development and deployment are imperative for building trust in AI systems and mitigating potential risks to individuals and communities.

Comprehensive data protection regulations, informed consent mechanisms, and privacy-preserving AI techniques are essential for upholding privacy rights in the context of AI applications. Additionally, promoting data transparency and empowering individuals with control over their data are fundamental principles in the ethical use of AI technologies.

AI Ethics and Standards

The establishment of AI ethics and standards involves collaborative efforts to define ethical principles, best practices, and industry standards that guide the responsible development and deployment of AI technologies. Ethical considerations in AI encompass fairness, accountability, transparency, and the societal impact of AI advancements.

Developing AI ethics frameworks and standards requires engagement with diverse stakeholders, including technologists, ethicists, policymakers, and the public, to ensure that AI technologies align with ethical norms and contribute to positive societal outcomes. Furthermore, promoting ethical AI education and fostering a culture of ethical awareness are essential for upholding ethical standards in the AI ecosystem.

Review Questions

1. What are the potential impacts of AI on employment and the workforce?

    A. Automation and Job Displacement

B. Cultural Diversity and Bias

C. New Job Opportunities

D. Workplace Transformation

2. Which of the following is a social and cultural implication of AI?

   A. Skill Development and Reskilling

   B. Ethical Decision-Making in AI

   C. AI Literacy and Curriculum Integration

   D. Regulation and Accountability

3. What is an important aspect of education and training related to AI?

   A. Privacy and Data Protection

   B. Regulation and Accountability

   C. Automation and Job Displacement

   D. AI Literacy and Curriculum Integration

4. Which area is addressed by public policy and governance in the context of AI?

   A. Automation and Job Displacement

   B. AI Literacy and Curriculum Integration

   C. New Job Opportunities

   D. Regulation and Accountability

5. What is a key consideration in the context of AI and society?

    A. Cultural Diversity and Bias

    B. AI in Educational Technology

    C. AI Ethics and Standards

    D. Human-AI Collaboration

Explore AI, its benefits, and what the future has to offer. I think you will be amazed!

www.ingramcontent.com/pod-product-compliance
Lightning Source LLC
LaVergne TN
LVHW051735050326
832903LV00023B/934